MW00784720

Horse Training In-Hand

A Modern Guide to Working from the Ground

WORK ON THE LONGE

LONG LINES

SHORT AND LONG REINS

Ellen Schuthof-Lesmeister
and Kip Mistral

Foreword by Sylvia Loch

*Featuring Hand-Drawn Illustrations
by Ellen Schuthof-Lesmeister*

TRAFALGAR SQUARE
North Pomfret, Vermont

First published in 2009 by
Trafalgar Square Books
North Pomfret, Vermont 05053

Printed in China

Library of Congress Cataloging-in-Publication Data

Schuthof-Lesmeister, Ellen.
  Horse training in-hand : a modern guide to working from the ground · Work on the longe · Long lines · Long and short reins /Ellen Schuthof-Lesmeister & Kip Mistral.
    p. cm.
  Includes bibliographical references and index.
  ISBN 978-1-57076-409-7 (alk. paper)
  1. Horses--Training. 2. Long reining (Horsemanship) I. Mistral, Kip. II. Title.
  SF287.S88 2009
  636.1'0835--dc22
                          2009002362

Photo credits: The following photographs were taken by Kip Mistral: 1.4, 1.5, 1.7, 1.8, 1.9, 1.12, 1.13, 1.14, 1.15, 2.1, 2.8, 2.9, 2.12, 2.13, 2.15, 2.16, 3.1, 3.2, 3.3, 4.12 A & B, 4.38 A & B, 5.7, 5.11, 5.15, 5.22 A–C, 5.23 B, 5.28. All others are courtesy of Stal Paradiso.

Book design by Carrie Fradkin
Jacket design by Heather Mansfield
Typefaces: Scala, Scala Sans. Trade Gothic

10 9 8 7 6 5 4 3 2

Dedication

"Work in-hand is the basis for everything. Without an understanding of work-in hand, riders will reach a plateau that only additional force can move them off. With knowledge of work in-hand, understanding replaces force and lightness begins. Unfortunately most riders start their training astride, and to get off the horse to learn to ride seems counter-intuitive. But one MUST practice work-in hand to ride well, because once astride our legs and seat so easily overpower what our other aids tell the horse. It is amazing how few riders will take the time to even consider this most important part of the art, and how few even know about it. Yet, without work in-hand it is impossible to make that first gentle whispering connection with the horse. Horses are SO surprised when you begin work in-hand with them; every horse knows it from the moment they are born. They are mystified that we humans know it too. And they love it when we do. Once work in-hand is practiced, once you are astride, you and your horse have a common language and a conversation can begin."

—JOSEPH BERTO, STUDENT OF BETTINA DRUMMOND

Contents

Foreword

The discipline of *working the horse from the ground* is steeped in history. The first mention of this work as a serious art appears in King Dom Duarte of Portugal's book *Livro da Ensinanca de Bem Cavalgar* (1434). The first of the old Masters to introduce the use of pillars, his was an enlightened approach, treating the horse with respect and gentleness and always taking time at every stage of training.

In today's world, one might rue the absence of this work ethic or indeed the lack of detailed technical explanation available to today's would-be student. Few riding schools teach the work in hand, longeing is often not deemed worthy of a lesson and generally, one has to travel a long way to find an instructor of caliber. Even in the realm of equestrian literature, there is—except in a couple of cases—a dearth of helpful information. Few manuals thoroughly address the difficulties and intricacies of training a horse or allow for the fact that things don't always go to plan: the very nature of horses is often overlooked with much importance placed on subscribing to a general pattern of training that may not necessarily advance at the same pace with every horse.

Riding out in the countryside and the evolution from manège riding to competitive sport has no doubt contributed to this attitude. How refreshing therefore to find in Schuthof-Lesmeister and Mistral's book, such a wonderfully in-depth, yet truly riveting coverage of the reasons behind training in-hand as well as how to do it properly! Here we find meaningful background to the subject, which not only gives the reader confidence to proceed but then gives him or her every reason to proceed.

The *work in-hand on the short rein* is always hugely admired when academies such as the Spanish Riding School of Vienna or the Royal Andalusian School of Equestrian Art come to town, but it has often retained a daunting image for the many riders who would like to know more. Even those true Master horsemen and women who practice it—and there are still a good number in the Iberian Peninsula—may not be so proficient at teaching it. I well remember my own frustration when starting this work back in 1970s Portugal, I was told to watch and copy—but never told *how*.

In *Horse Training In-Hand*, we discover in Ellen an instructor who is not only willing to share all the techniques, the subtleties and the ethos of her own beautifully presented work, but also her passion for the horse—for doing it right for him. With an impeccable classical background, she has obviously probed and explored her subject with an open mind and a willingness to learn from every experience, every horse. This book demonstrates her strengths as a trainer who really cares for her horses and whose understanding of the physical reality results in work that will be lasting and true. Her own, very unique way of putting this across is a delight to read.

When it comes to the *longe* and the *long rein work*, I have been repeatedly dismayed at the lack of knowledge witnessed at different stables or yards and with different "trainers." Longeing is often performed in a perfunctory manner, as though at best "to let the sparks fly," or at worst to "wear the horse out" before the rider then takes to the saddle. Often there is no attempt whatsoever to improve the gaits, or use body language to instil confidence, let alone to encourage natural spontaneity within the horse, which can reap so many benefits. What I love about this book is how it seeks to address all these issues as well as showing a deep understanding about sharing space, invisible pressure points and general leadership.

Having taught co-author Kip Mistral at my own manège at home in Scotland and having the privilege to know her over many a discussion both face-to-face and by email, I have always admired her commitment to classical riding. Her ability to stay focused and her attention to detail works extraordinarily well with such an artistic and sensitive nature. I have also been at the receiving end of her organizational skills, which included transporting me from Edinburgh to Los Angeles for a series of lectures and instructional days—but I have also seen the wistful, empathetic side of her that transforms itself into the handling of her own much loved horse and the caring for others around her.

Knowing Kip's depth of commitment, I am not surprised that this book has turned out to be a masterpiece of clarity and design. As she herself freely admits: "Being a technical writer, I wanted to create training modules that would describe as thoroughly as possible what to do and how to troubleshoot." This has indeed been achieved on a grand scale and in a very attractive format. I love all the white space and the extraordinarily beautiful photographs. In fact I have not been able to put the book down since I first had sight of it.

Particularly impressive is the devotion given to the preparation, the gathering of equipment, the safety angles of starting the work, plus of course the methodology itself. And here, in the main body of the book— the *modus operandi*—are treated to so much good, practical advice, it seems nothing short of a miracle that nothing has been left out. For readers who have never long-reined, never longed and never worked closely by their horse's shoulder, fear not! Skilfully, the authors will lead you through each important step, every procedure along the way.

Horse Training In-Hand is a book much needed by today's riders in today's world. Nicely sectioned into easily assimilated "lessons," this wonderful oeuvre can be picked up time and time again—its modules similar to that of a superior university course. To assist you on that journey, the illustrations are clear and concise, the layout clean and the photographs extremely explicit. As if that wasn't enough, the whole style is inviting and very readable.

In coming together with Kip Mistral, Ellen Schuthof-Lesmeister has happily discovered a fellow traveller in her journey with horses and how to understand them better. Master of Horsemanship meets Master of Expression and Explanation and it's a successful marriage resulting in a truly extraordinary and beautiful book.

Sylvia Loch
Eden Hall, Kelso, Scotland
www.classicalriding.co.uk

Preface

About Ellen Schuthof-Lesmeister

As an equestrian journalist, I feel the greatest pleasure when someone reads what I have written and contacts me to discuss it. It is my policy always to reply to these correspondents, and never have I been so richly rewarded than when I replied to Ellen Schuthof-Lesmeister's first email from the Netherlands. We began a wonderful dialogue and friendship that is now in its fourth year.

It has been a real inspiration to get to know this dynamic and original horsewoman. She was born with an uncommon passion for horses that accounts for her broad foundation in horsemanship. Ellen told me funny childhood stories about stealing rides on bareback ponies in the woods, and not-so-funny grownup stories about riding in Dutch jumping and dressage competition. Unhappy in grim competitive environments, Ellen began to daydream about riding a white baroque stallion in the light, elegant, classical style. And in what I now know as her hallmark, Ellen set forth with unwavering dedication to find a young Spanish stallion and then learn how to train him in the classical way.

She sought the best methods from the top classical trainers in Europe, a long "Who's Who" list spanning Spain, Portugal, France, Belgium, Germany, Denmark, and the Netherlands that would impress anyone. Ellen explained that throughout all her explorations, her quest had been to find gentle methods of handling and "training" a horse that condition him to be exquisitely light and flexible in the hand, whether on the ground or in the saddle. It is her love for the horse that pushed her to look at many different systems of horsemanship, and as she experimented, the responses of her horses showed her when she was doing something right. Everything she did, she did to win and keep the horse's trust. You rarely hear that kind of commitment from a horse trainer...and I was fascinated.

Then, with her characteristic generosity, Ellen invited me to visit her and her Andalusian stallions in Holland and even travel with them to Denmark for a summer academic equitation clinic. Of course I had no choice but to go! As I spent the first two weeks with Ellen and watched her with her stallions, I saw for myself that the result of her sensitive handling of them was a kind of horse-human relationship of such reciprocal love, admiration, and trust that it is—in my view—unequalled. Since then, not only has her classical horsemanship attracted attention in Holland and nearby countries, her unique rapport with horses has become my ideal.

A "true horseman" reaches a certain level as a thinking person, and whatever his or her equestrian background, develops empathy for the horse itself. In Ellen's opinion, we expect the impossible when we assume we can have a fully-trained horse by the time he is seven years old. Her focus is to build a strong and supple horse, and she does this with months and years of gymnastic exercises on the ground.

"Human bodybuilders take five to 10 years to develop their muscles," Ellen says. "Making muscle requires hormones, and the body can produce only so much hormone every day. So, it takes years of constant work to build the desired layers of muscle. It is the same with horses."

If you allow your horse time to steadily increase his confidence and you keep his training periods short, he will enjoy the challenges of his work with you. Horses can become stressed, weary, frustrated, and bored with the typical long, tiring, 45- to 60-minute training session. Instead, your goal should be to end each lesson with an energetic, proud horse that wants to please you. To Ellen, force is *never* connected with happiness. If your horse's training process takes a natural course where the horse is constantly supported but never forced beyond his capabilities, one day he will *offer* you collection. When he is happy, healthy, strong, balanced, and relaxed, your horse will dance—like Ellen's do.

About This Book

Although most of Ellen's background is in dressage, she thinks of the term *dressage* (derived from the French verb *dresser*, meaning *to train*) in the broad way that it was originally intended. *Dressage training* is meant to develop the horse physically and mentally. It begins the moment you begin training a horse, making him into an athlete that is strong, balanced, and ready to help you pursue any equestrian discipline.

In this book, we describe techniques for work *in-hand*, which, when executed properly, will greatly contribute to a flexible, strong, "light" horse and provide an excellent foundation for all future work. These progressive in-hand lessons include basic longeing and double-longeing, long-lining, and work in the short reins and long reins. Although I am contributing my own knowledge and experience to this book in the writing of it, this book is about Ellen's training methods and the voice is hers.

Both Ellen and I feel that many training books assume a high level of experience and expertise, often confusing beginners, and we want Ellen's training techniques to be accessible to everyone. Therefore, we broke each type of work in-hand into elementary lessons. Each lesson contains background, theory, process, and procedures, as well as drawings and photographs. It is our hope that you will take this book down to the arena—or wherever you and your horse work together—start at the very beginning, and work through to the very end.

Kip Mistral

PART I

Orientation to Work In-Hand

On the pages that follow, please find some of the terms I use throughout this book. Many of these words may be familiar, and indeed, you may understand them to mean something slightly different than how I describe them here. However, for clarity's sake, this is how I choose to define them for the purposes of training horses in-hand and the lessons to come later.

Balance   Total ability of a horse to be equally supple and strong on both sides of his body, so that he can be straight. There is no balance without straightness (see **Straight/ness**).

Bend/ing   Ability of a horse to flex his body from poll to tail in either direction in a correct manner; provides stretching and suppling exercise.

Changing rein   Changing direction. When you are on the "right rein," you are traveling to the right—for example, making a circle to the right. When you "change rein," you change direction, making a circle to the left, and you are now on the "left rein."

Collection   When a horse is so gymnasticized, strong, and supple that he can literally raise his back, and flex and lower his hindquarters, and sustain this posture as required during work in-hand or under saddle, he is said to be *collected*. Also referred to as "self-carriage." In true collection, the forehand of the horse appears as if it is rising, but in actuality, his hindquarters are lowered. There is no true collection without straightness (see **Straight/ness**).

Driving hand/arm   In work in-hand, this is the hand that holds the whip, or performs the action of the "leg aid," for example pressing against the horse's body to ask him to yield.

Exercise   A specific lesson, such as shoulder-in, renvers, travers, yield to the "leg," or half-pass, that requires the horse to physically master certain gymnastic requirements and also mentally understand what is being asked of him.

Flexion   Can be used in reference to the limbs, as when a joint angle becomes smaller (as in *flexion of the haunches*), or in reference to the *longitudinal flexion* at the poll (the chin moves away from or toward the underside of the neck), *lateral flexion* of the neck and poll (movement of the head from left to right), as well as the spine as a whole (*flexibility* allows bend).

Forehand   The horse's head, neck, and shoulders. Most of a horse's weight is *naturally* carried on his forehand. The common phrase "on the forehand" refers to the way horses move when they are young, early in their training, or improperly trained.

Forward and down   A horse should be worked "forward and down" (also known as "long and low") as part of a correct training program. This posture relaxes his back and enables the back muscles to move freely.

Gymnastics   A training program comprised of bending, stretching, suppling, and strengthening exercises.

"Inside/outside" the bend or circle   The "inside" or "outside" is not always determined by which side of the horse is closest to the rail, and which is closest to the center of the ring. Often, when I refer to the "inside" or "outside," I'm referring to the horse's bend: the direction of the bend determines which part of his body is "inside" the movement or "outside" the movement. For instance, when the horse is bending to the left, his left side is "inside" and his right "outside," regardless of where you are positioned in the arena. The muscles in the horse's body inside the bend are shortened, and the muscles on the outside are stretched.

Inside track   The path adjacent to the *track*, toward the inside of the arena (see also **Track**, and further explanation on p. 80).

Lateral movement   Going forward and sideways simultaneously. Work in-hand uses lateral movements to supple and strengthen the horse.

Leading hand/arm   In work in-hand, this is the hand that guides the horse. You hold the lead line, longe line, or rein in this hand, and sometimes "point" in the direction you want to go. For example, when you longe the horse to the left, your left hand is the leading hand.

Long side   In an arena of traditional rectangular proportions, this refers to the longer side of the rectangle.

Movement   In this book, when I use the term *movement*, I am referring to the motion related to a horse traveling in one direction or another. The in-hand exercises I use work with the horse's movement to train and gymnasticize specific parts of his body.

Point of weight   The horse's center of balance where he "carries" both his own weight and that of the rider is a point located behind the withers. A horse needs to be supple and strong enough to bring his hind legs underneath himself and toward that point in order to support this weight correctly. This is the goal of attaining self-carriage.

Relaxation   The absence of stress and tightness in a horse's body, which is optimal for free, correct movement. However, this kind of relaxation is not without a certain amount of "positive tension" that keeps tone in the muscles.

Short side   In an arena of traditional rectangular proportions, this refers to the shorter side of the rectangle.

Straight/ness   The ability of a horse to move straight ahead on lines and bend along the arc of curves with rhythmic, balanced gaits and his hind feet stepping into the tracks of the front, and without favoring one side over the other. Keep in mind that, like humans, horses are naturally "right-" or "left-handed," and because of this, keeping a horse *straight* is a continual process that spans his lifetime.

Strength/en One of the goals of work in-hand is a *strong* horse, and the exercises to come aim to strengthen his muscles in his back, legs, and hindquarters.

Supple/ness Flexibility that results from bending and stretching exercises.

Track This term has multiple definitions. It is used to describe the path closest to the rail, wall, or arena fence. It also refers to lateral movements and the number of directions the horse is moving in: single-track (forward) or two-track (forward and sideways). In addition, it describes the number of legs you can see if you stand directly in front of the horse as he is moving toward you (i.e., the horse is moving on two tracks, three tracks, or four).

WHAT IT MEANS TO WORK IN-HAND

The term *work in-hand* simply means that the handler trains the horse from the ground as opposed to riding him. In its broadest meaning, it refers to the entire training spectrum, from teaching a foal to lead all the way up to perfecting airs above the ground in the haute école.

This book describes five types of in-hand groundwork, which, when taught consecutively, act as building blocks. You will begin with *basic longeing* and *double-longeing,* progress through *long-lining* and *short-reining,* and finally achieve the "crown jewel" of work in-hand: *long-reining* (see more information about each of these beginning on p. 14). Keep in mind that different horses may respond better to one type of in-hand work than others. For instance, a horse that works well in short reins may not be as responsive in long reins. You will need to be observant and adjust your lessons accordingly.

In-hand work is an ideal training methodology to use when:

- Starting a green or young horse
- Restarting a horse that needs remedial training

- Working a horse that needs therapeutic physical exercise and cannot be ridden
- Keeping an older horse that shouldn't be ridden often—or at all—strong and fit
- Keeping a horse trained and conditioned even when a trainer can't ride, perhaps due to injury
- Demonstrating lateral exercises from the ground to a student in the saddle, so that the student can feel the horse's movement without being distracted by trying to give the correct aids (photos 1.1 A–D)
- Giving variation to the training program of the horse (and trainer)
- Warming up a saddled horse before riding

A   B   C   D

The ultimate goal of this groundwork is to help the horse attain *lightness* and *self-carriage*, where he is balanced on both sides of his body, moves straight in both directions on lines and curves, and is strong and supple. When he can sustain the optimal degree of collection, he will be able to support not only his own weight but carry yours correctly and efficiently, helping him stay sound over his lifetime and be an overall joy to ride.

1.1 A–D One of the many benefits of in-hand work is the teaching opportunity it presents. Here I am showing a student what it feels like to move laterally. Since she is not distracted by trying to give the correct aids, she can concentrate on the horse's movement—telling me when his front legs are crossing, when his hind legs are crossing, and sensing the shift of his hindquarters as we move from a left to a right bend.

Benefits for the Horse and Handler

Mastering work in-hand contributes significantly to the horse's athleticism and the handler's expertise as a trainer.

Benefits for the Horse

In-hand exercises prepare a horse both *physically* and *mentally* to perform movements as requested in a timely and correct manner.

Physically, in-hand work improves the athleticism of any horse, any age, because it is *gymnastic*. For example, work on the longe line in easy, large circles strengthens and conditions the horse, providing a foundation of fitness and balance and thus enabling him to benefit from the more challenging short-rein and long-rein exercises. Carefully controlled *lateral* exercises (such as Yield to the "Leg," see p. 96) encourage the horse to *stretch* and *bend* on both sides of his body. The accumulated work of slow, progressive stretching and bending exercises give the horse flexibility and suppleness, and ultimately result in his ability to become truly *straight* for short periods. Plus, when you stretch his muscles slowly and over time as in my in-hand lessons, the horse is more physically comfortable during the exercises, creating positive experiences that lead to him welcoming such work in the future.

Mentally, a horse benefits from work in-hand because he understands he should be obedient to the handler's aids, which are essentially the same as those given from the saddle. When mounted, the horse will be familiar with the aids a rider employs. In addition, the horse learns to focus on progressively more challenging work.

Benefits for the Handler

Anyone can learn how to use in-hand work because the physical skills involved on the handler's part are basic. You must walk, sometimes jog beside the horse, and use simple physical coordination. This gives you an opportunity to improve your own physical condition and coordination while at the same time training your horse.

In this book, each new lesson builds on the one you have taught previously and prepares you for the one you will teach next, creating a smooth learning curve. In no time, you'll be progressing alongside your horse from the elementary to the advanced.

THE ELEMENTS OF BALANCE

A horse's ability to carry himself well depends mainly on his *lateral suppleness* as well as the *suppleness and strength of his back*. Both of these are consciously addressed in all five types of work in-hand I describe. However, before you learn to use the lessons that improve lateral suppleness and back strength, it is important to understand the common problems specific to these areas.

Lateral Suppleness

Every horse has a "stiff" side and a more "supple" side (we might say he is "right-" or "left-handed"). Typically, his stiff side is his left side. Horsemen's myths reason that the foal grows in his mother's womb curled to the left, or even that a horse's stiff side is the side where his mane naturally lays flat. Research in human genetics indicates that right-handedness and left-handedness is inherited, so it may be this way with horses, too. In addition, we may encourage stiffness on the left because we traditionally handle horses from that side.

Myths aside, when a horse obviously favors bending his neck and body in one direction—whether due to birth position, compensation for an injury, or having been trained or ridden incorrectly—he has actually *contracted* the muscles on this "bendable" side. It becomes stiff and tight, while at the same time, the *other* side of the horse is stretched and supple because it ends up doing most of the work. For instance, when your horse "favors" the left, and you ask him to bend right, the contracted muscles on his left side will have a difficult time complying. And if the horse is uncomfortable enough, he may evade bending to the right. When people say, "My horse *won't* take his right lead," in truth he probably *can't* take his right lead and keep the compensatory balance that he has developed over time. (See more about stiff and supple sides on p. 36.)

SYMPTOMS OF LATERAL IMBALANCE

Signs of *lateral imbalance* (extreme "left-" or "right-handedness") include, but are not limited to, the following:

- When working the horse in a circle on his stiff side, the foreleg on his supple side reaches forward normally, while the foreleg on the stiff side comes up short. When the stiffness is pronounced, the horse may even appear to "hop" on that foreleg, as if he has a "peg-leg."

- When sitting on the horse and looking down at his shoulders, one side is obviously more developed and larger than the other. (The underdeveloped side is the stiff side.)

- When riding the horse, you feel that you must constantly readjust your weight toward one side. This could mean that his stiff, less developed—and therefore weak—side is "dropping" instead of holding up his (and your) weight to the same degree as the supple, stronger side of his body. Proof may be seen on your saddle pad after the horse works up a light sweat: even when the saddle fits the horse's back perfectly, there will be a darker impression of sweat and dirt on one side of the pad than the other. This indicates your weight is pressing down more on the stiff, weak side of the horse's body because it is constantly dropping.

Note: A handler may find that he is more strongly left- or right-oriented than he realized (unless he is a dancer!), and discover that like the horse, he feels more awkward when working on one side of his body than the other. Learning work in-hand is an excellent opportunity for the one-sided handler to fine-tune his coordination.

Suppleness and Strength of the Back

A horse at liberty naturally moves mostly on his forehand, unless he wishes, for example, to show off—any horse may demonstrate collection when prancing up to another horse to exchange greetings. A stallion will magnificently collect himself to impress a mare. However, these beautiful, natural moments of "self-carriage" are fleeting and do not require sustained strength.

It is a different matter for a horse in training. In order for a horse to carry himself, great amounts of strength and suppleness along the topline and torso are required.

In his book *Tug of War: Classical Versus "Modern" Dressage* (Trafalgar Square Books, 2007), author and veterinarian Dr. Gerd Heuschmann explains that a young horse (although this applies to *any* undeveloped or poorly trained horse) being ridden forward and downward correctly can carry himself and his rider for a *short* period using the nuchal ligament in his neck to raise his back and allow it to "swing." The notion of a "swinging" back is one that many of us are familiar with—we want our horse to exhibit a springy motion with each thrust off his hind legs transmitted through his topline by trunk muscles that actively contract and release, neither remaining rigid nor slack. However, Dr.

Heuschmann goes on to say that after 15 to 20 minutes, the horse's neck mechanism tires, and he lifts his head and neck to relax those muscles. This causes his back to drop, and tense up under the burden of carrying his own weight and that of his rider.

When the back is tense, other muscle systems also tense. Under these conditions of tension, discomfort, and perhaps even spasm, the "swinging" sensation is lost and the rhythm of all the gaits suffers. Plus, the horse whose back is unprotected by a strong and supple musculature will almost certainly suffer spinal damage, because the spine takes all the weight of the rider's body and tack without support from the rest of his body.

The point is, a horse that does not have strong stomach muscles cannot contract them to raise his back, keep it supple, and eventually collect himself with a rider (photo 1.2). Short periods of work forward and downward may allow the back to raise temporarily, as described above, but until a horse is properly physically prepared, it is impossible to attain any semblance of collection. Here's where work in-hand can be of infinite value: Dr. Heuschmann states unequivocally that preparing a young horse as a riding horse requires one-and-a-half to two years of "solid, unspectacular gymnastic work"—over time, the significant suppling and strengthening achievable with work in-hand collects the horse from the ground providing an ideal foundation for safe, correct mounted work. A truly collected horse—one that has a strong, supple back and supportive stomach—is a pleasure to ride.

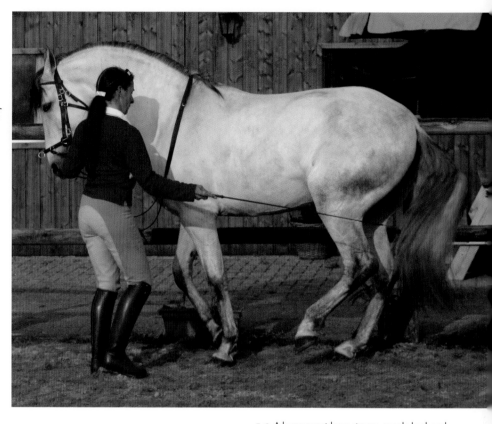

1.2 A horse must have strong, supple back and stomach muscles. These allow him to raise his back—as you can see Fernando doing here—and eventually correctly support a rider. Fernando naturally has a difficult time lowering his hindquarters and bringing his hind legs under him due to his conformation, but after four years of consistent work in-hand, he has acquired the muscular strength and conditioning to offer the piaffe.

WHEN TO BEGIN WORK IN-HAND

One must consider both the horse's physical state and mental disposition when determining whether he is capable of the groundwork exercises described in this book. Obviously, in the case of young horses, maturity is an issue. *Do not attempt to longe a horse under two years old, and do not begin lateral work in-hand with a horse under three.* I believe that work in-hand is an excellent place to start a young horse. However, the bending involved in longeing in circles, and the sideways movement required in lateral exercises, are severe on growing joints. I also feel that the amount of focus required for much of the work in-hand is really too much for the mind of a horse younger than three years.

One school of thought believes work in-hand should not be attempted before the horse can be ridden correctly in the same exercises. For some horses that might be true—for instance, a more excitable type of horse, and some stallions, can often be handled more easily from the saddle than on the ground. (A few of these horses will probably *never* be good candidates for work in-hand.) However, I believe the majority of horses can begin initial training on the longe line at two years old (only on large circles to prevent straining the joints and ligaments), and progress slowly and according to the individual's physical and mental development from there. Older horses in need of remedial training or extra conditioning work can begin work in-hand at any time. As always, the horse's health and soundness should be of primary concern when beginning and carrying out any training program.

In addition, anatomical issues require consideration when you begin work in-hand (or in fact *any* kind of horse training). Among the most important of these are (1) your horse's physical conformation and how that will affect his natural ability to collect himself, and (2) your horse's head and mouth conformation and how that will affect his ability to flex his poll and the bit(s) that are appropriate for him as together you progress through the work in-hand exercises.

Conformation, Collection, and Flexion

The horse's conformation has a critical effect on his ability to collect himself. *Collection* always starts from behind—the flexing and lowering of the hindquarters that takes place makes it appear as if the forehand is "rising" as the horse bears more weight behind, counteracting the fact that horses naturally move on their forehand most of the time (see also p. 40).

Certain conformation exaggerates the natural tendency to move on the forehand. For instance, my stallion Pícaro has a very heavy neck and a steep shoulder, so he naturally moves on his forehand and takes short steps. It is a challenge for him to bring his hindquarters under and shift his weight from front to back—he likes to stay on his forehand since it is easier for him.

It is logical that when the horse is built "downhill," meaning that his hips are higher than his withers, collection will be difficult. (Note: when the horse is built "uphill," with his withers higher than his hips, it may *appear* that his hindquarters are flexed and dropped, but this is an illusion. The horse is still actually carrying himself on his forehand. It will, however, be easier to train him to transfer weight from his forehand to his hind end.) Further, if his hind legs are "camped out" behind, he will have a hard time bringing them underneath his body. A horse with a long-bodied conformation will have a tendency to *push* with his hind end rather than *carry* with it—my stallion Fernando has a long body, high hindquarters, and takes long steps (see photo 1.2, p. 11). In his early in-hand training, he was generally weak in all his muscles and produced a very strong "pushing" trot instead of carrying his weight properly by stepping under himself with his hind legs. He cantered so heavily on his forehand that his nose practically touched the ground. However, four years of work in-hand (and additional mounted training), with lots of lateral exercises, conditioned him to use his hind end correctly.

Flexion (longitudinal) is the horse's ability to raise his neck from his shoulders and flex his poll, bringing his chin toward the underside of his neck so that his profile is slightly in front of or at the vertical. (Note: *lateral* flexion is movement of the neck and poll from left to right.) A horse may be able to flex his poll naturally to a degree, but his ability to bring his head near the vertical, depends again on conformation. In this case, it matters how much space he has anatomically between the point where his jawbone ends and the point where the front of his neck begins. With proper training, the range of a horse's flexion can be tremendously increased, even when conformation gets in the way.

LONGE OR LONG? LINE OR REIN?

You may be confused by the admittedly similar terms *longe line, long line,* and *long rein*. I use all three at different phases throughout the book. I discuss equipment beginning on p. 18, which will shed further light on the subject, but here are some basics to help you understand my descriptions of the five types of in-hand work:

- Basic longeing and double-longeing utilize *longe lines* (first one, and then two in the case of double-longeing—see p. 33), while the horse moves around the handler on the circle.

- Although called *long-lining*, this next phase (which sequentially follows double-longeing) also utilizes two longe lines. The main difference is now the handler walks at some distance behind the horse, actually "driving" him. (Note: some people do use driving reins when long-lining, but I find they tend to be too heavy for work in hand.)

- Finally, *long reins* are simply elongated versions of regular bridle reins, and when using them, the handler walks on either side of the horse, at his hip, or in the style of the Spanish Riding School, immediately behind the horse.

So, keep in mind that although every horse benefits from work in-hand, your horse's conformation is a primary consideration as you progress through the lessons. *Know your horse* and his physical needs and limitations before you begin; understanding how and when an exercise may be difficult for him will help you, help him, as you go.

DEFINING THE TYPES OF WORK IN-HAND

The types of work I discuss in this book are defined below in the order they should be undertaken. Only when you and your horse have mastered one should you progress to the next. This practice keeps the learning curve consistent and ensures that you and your horse stay confident.

- Basic longeing
- Double-longeing
- Long-lining
- Work in short reins
- Work in long reins

1 Basic Longeing (p. 34)

In *basic longeing,* the horse wears a cavesson and/or a bridle and side reins (see p. 24), and travels in a circle around the trainer at the walk, trot, and canter in both directions (photo 1.3). Longeing encourages the horse to be obedient; work calmly and with relaxation; learn to move with rhythm; loosen, stretch, and supple his muscles; and balance both sides of his body. When properly used, side reins teach him to reach for a soft contact with the bit and help him learn to use both sides of his body in balance.

2 Double-Longeing (p. 56)

As the bridge between basic longeing on the circle and long-lining, *double-longeing* is an art form in itself (photo 1.4). Again, a cavesson and/or bridle and side reins are used, and the horse travels in a circle around the trainer at the walk, trot, and canter in both directions. However, this time two longe lines are employed instead of one. Mastering this exercise prepares the horse for the long lines.

3 Long-Lining (p. 69)

When you *long line* a horse, he wears a cavesson and/or bridle and side reins, and you walk *behind* him at the end of two longe lines (photo 1.5). It looks the same as if you were driving the horse in a cart or buggy. Lessons include halt, walk, trot, rein-back, changes of direction, and figure eights. The goal is to establish control, as you are communicating with the horse from a distance, and from behind. Once the horse is attentive and obedient on the long lines, you may be ready to step up yet another level to work with the short reins.

4 Work in Short Reins (p. 79)

Short reins are simply ordinary bridle reins. For a green horse, you can use two sets of reins: one attached to the side rings of the working cavesson and one to the bit. This way, he can

1.3 When longeing, the horse travels around the handler at a walk, trot, or canter. The handler controls the horse via a long cotton line clipped to a cavesson.

1.4 Similar to basic longeing, double-longeing requires the horse move in a circle around the handler at the walk, trot, or canter; however, the handler now employs two longe lines—one on either side of the horse—rather than one.

1.5 Long-lining is a natural progression from double-longeing. Now, using two longe lines, the handler walks at some distance behind the horse and teaches the horse rein aids and basic school figures while establishing control.

1.6 Work in short reins allows you to ask the horse for various lateral movements while you position yourself at his head, neck, shoulder, or side. You work from both sides of the horse—here I work on the right rein with one of my more advanced horses outfitted in a leverage bit and two sets of short reins.

begin to become accustomed to the action of the reins on the bit while you still rely on the cavesson, which he is used to from his work on the longe line(s). Eventually, your goal is to remove the cavesson and graduate to a single set of short reins attached to the bit. More advanced work in-hand may use two sets of reins attached to a bit or bits, as in a double bridle or leverage bit such as the one I'm using in photo 1.6.

During short rein exercises you walk beside the horse, positioning yourself at his head, neck, or shoulder, and sometimes his side. Your horse will stretch his shoulders and free his ribs; step under himself to strengthen his hindquarters; supple and straighten his whole body in preparation for collection; and learn obedience to you as he learns to yield his body willingly. On the short reins you can teach shoulder-in, leg-yield, half-pass, renvers, travers, piaffe, up through the haute école.

5 Work in Long Reins (p. 143)

It is a natural step to progress from the short reins to *long reins*. Long reins are simply elongated versions of the short reins—although you only use *one* pair of long reins—and any movement your horse learned on the long lines and short reins can be practiced (photo 1.7). In some ways, long reins are easier to use than short reins: they are more convenient because you can easily change direction while on the move, whereas short reins require you stop the horse and change sides. Also, a sensitive horse may feel too much pressure when a handler works at his shoulder as in short reins and may work better in long reins when the handler is some distance from his head. There

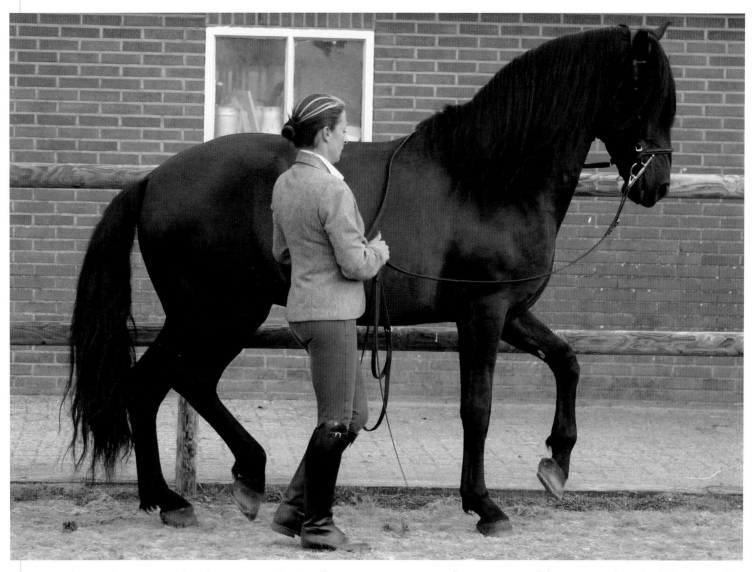

is an inherent danger to work in long reins as the handler's position is close to the hindquarters and in kicking range. At the same time, the horse proves his obedience when he obeys his handler from this position.

1.7 Long reins allow you to practice all the exercises you learned in the long lines and short reins, but your position further tests the horse's obedience and sensitivity. This stallion responds to the lightest of rein aids as you can see by my easy contact and position back near his hip.

CORRECT EQUIPMENT FOR WORK IN-HAND

My goal is to use the least amount of tack and equipment possible when I train horses; the more cooperative, obedient, and well-trained the horse, the less I will need. The smaller the space I use for training, the more control I have over the horse merely with my presence and energy—another variable that impacts the amount and type of equipment necessary. For example, in an enclosed arena of limited proportions, I may choose not to use side reins because the horse feels secure in the workspace and does not need the extra stability provided by this training aid. However, when training a young stallion or a green horse in a large, fairly open field, I may need side reins both for the horse's state of mind and for my own safety.

Depending on your horse and your own expertise, keep in mind that the more tack you put on the horse to control him, the more ways you can potentially damage him physically, and even psychologically. *Partnership* and *lightness* are always your goals.

Workspace and Basic Equipment

Here is a list of what you need for working a horse in-hand. Examine the photos and see how each piece is placed on the horse, and read the descriptions that explain the principles involved.

- Arena with proper footing
- Working cavesson
- Bridle with full-cheek snaffle or ring snaffle (a full-cheek snaffle is preferred for longeing and long-lining—see also my discussion of bits, p. 21)
- Two, 25-foot cotton longe lines
- Two pairs short reins
- One pair long reins
- Surcingle with multiple rings
- One pair side reins—plain leather (no elastic)

- One each: dressage, carriage, and longe whip
- Sturdy gloves
- Boots or proper protective footwear

Arenas and Footing

I encourage you to work your horse in-hand in whatever safe, enclosed area you have available. If you have round pens and arenas of different sizes to work with, make use of them! The horse usually feels "safer" in a smaller arena, but more "free" (yet at the same time potentially less secure) in a larger arena. Use every opportunity you can, taking baby steps, to encourage him to feel sure of you in whichever workspace you use.

The ideal is an arena with flat, absorbent footing that isn't too deep, and a solid border fence or wall. The dimensions should be at least 50 by 50 feet to allow room for large circles and changes of direction. Later in training, you may want to work your horse in a grassy field or pasture to change the scenery, alleviate boredom, and present him with new challenges in footing and distractions.

With regard to footing, it is popular, or perhaps merely simple, to have arenas and round pens with deep footing of organic material, such as manure compost or sand. Deep sand, in particular, is very bad for any horse—nothing strains his legs more than circling on the longe line in deep footing, and lateral movements in these scenarios put excessive pressure on the joints. Of course, worst of all is riding in it.

Every horse, young or old, needs good footing if his legs are to stay sound. I am so concerned about this that I had my outdoor arena prepared and surfaced in a special way. All the dirt was removed, to a depth of 13 inches. Then six trenches were dug for French drains to carry water away, and the drains were installed with a layer of volcanic rock between and over them. These drain to a channel outside the arena. Over this I have a flat layer of treated sand, which is mixed with pale green strands of manmade fiber. This wonderful footing—which is always perfect—continually amazes me. There is never any standing water (even in Holland, where it rains year-round!), the material stays in place, and it is soft and resilient for horses and humans to work in because we don't sink down into it.

1.8 Fernando wears the type of working cavesson I favor, ready for basic longeing. Also note the cheek strap which, when also fitted snugly, keeps the cavesson correctly positioned on the horse's head even when pulled on by a lead, line, or rein.

1.9 Pícaro is correctly outfitted in a cavesson and a bridle with full-cheek snaffle.

Working Cavesson

A halter is not secure or precise enough for any of the work in-hand that I teach. It is critical to choose a quality working cavesson with three rings on the nosepiece—it is an investment that will reward you throughout your equestrian career. I use a version of the French working cavesson with a nosepiece made of leather-covered bicycle chain (photo 1.8). When fitted correctly, it molds to the horse's nose more comfortably than one made of solid metal, yet it holds the horse's attention with firm pressure. (You can use a piece of sheepskin under the nosepiece for maximum comfort, although your horse will likely be more responsive without it.) I also find it encourages correct bending because you can precisely lead and flex the horse's head, poll, and neck from the front of his nose (rather than the side of his head, as you do with a bit). Above all, this type of working cavesson provides the necessary stability to deliver correct aids for all of my in-hand exercises.

Acquaint the horse with the pressure of the cavesson in a safe, quiet, enclosed area before you attempt your first exercise. It should be adjusted snugly on the head so it does not slip, and must be positioned so the nosepiece fits fully on the nasal bone, never down on the cartilage below. Adjust it higher than you think it should be. It will stretch during the work due to the moderate weight of the nosepiece and your pull on the rings.

Bridle with Full-Cheek Snaffle

I prefer a bridle with a full-cheek snaffle for in-hand work because the shape of this bit prevents it from sliding through the horse's mouth (photo 1.9). Fasten the cavesson *under* the bridle. In particular, the cavesson's noseband must always be fastened under the bridle.

Two, 25-Foot Cotton Longe Lines

In photo 1.3 (p. 15), I am longeing Fernando using the standard cotton longe line I prefer for in-hand work. You will need two, at least 25 feet in length, and they should not have chains on the clip end, nor should they have rubber "donuts" on the handler's end. You will use these longe lines for longeing, double-longeing, and long-lining exercises.

Two Pairs of Short Reins

When I train in the short reins, I often begin by using one set of reins attached to the cavesson to prevent overuse of those attached to the snaffle (photo 1.10). You want to protect the delicacy of the horse's mouth so lightness is possible. (Purists do not even lead the horse by the bridle.) The set of reins attached to the cavesson also helps encourage correct bending of the horse's head and neck. As training progresses, you can eventually move to only one set of reins attached to the bit.

1.10 Tanguillo wears a cavesson and bridle with a full-cheek snaffle, each correctly fitted with bridle reins for short rein in-hand work.

One Pair of Long Reins

Long reins are simply long versions of the standard bridle reins (photo 1.11). The can be attached to the cavesson or the bit, depending on the level of the horse's training.

Surcingle

I prefer a leather surcingle with multiple rings for guiding lines and reins, and adjusting the height of side reins when they are being used (photo 1.12). Of the many surcingles on the market, few are made of leather today, and many are made of nylon

THE HORSE'S MOUTH AND THE RIGHT BIT

The mouth is the telephone line between the horse and human, and your horse's teeth, tongue, and gums must be healthy and undamaged if your horse is to be relaxed, soft, and responsive in the bridle. In addition, some horses have a mouth of an unusual shape that requires special attention to the way you configure the bridle and bit.

The horse has large salivary glands in the throat area between the jaw and neck, which can become full and hard, causing him to be stiff in his poll area and unable to flex completely. When the horse makes a chewing action, the glands soften and release backed-up saliva into the mouth. The horse finds it easier to flex at his poll when this happens, which is one of the reasons why it is positive when a horse chews lightly on the bit.

I take all of the above into consideration when outfitting a horse with a bit for in-hand training. I want the bit to be the right size and shape to accommodate the horse's mouth, tongue, and head conformation. He should be comfortable and encouraged to mouth the bit slightly. For a young horse carrying a bit for the first time, I find a full-cheek snaffle (the cheek pieces prevent the bit from being pulled through the mouth), combined with a working cavesson to limit interaction with that sensitive mouth, is the best choice. The mouthpiece can be double-jointed, which is often easier for the horse to accept and hold in his mouth, or single-jointed, which I feel tends to stay more stable in the mouth. Although I prefer the full-cheek versions, eggbutt and loose-ring snaffles are also appropriate for work in-hand.

Note: if you have any doubts about the health of your horse's mouth, or any questions about its conformation, consult an equine dental professional or a veterinarian prior to beginning this training program.

1.11 Fernando is outfitted in the cavesson, bridle, and long reins (he also has on a surcingle, see photo 1.12).

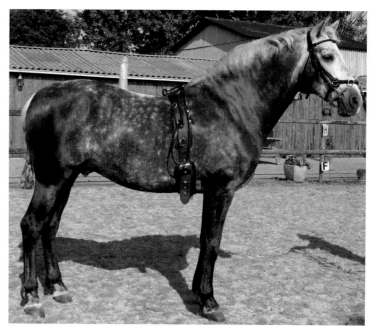

1.12 Pícaro wears a correctly positioned neoprene surcingle with the side reins (see p. 24) clipped up and out of the way, as I describe in photo 1.14, p. 24.

webbing, which has no give. The best solution I have found is a surcingle with a padded Neoprene lining and a leather top layer. Note: some horses are allergic to Neoprene, so watch for skin sensitivity.

The surcingle is the precursor for the saddle and girth. If you are lucky enough to be the person to "girth" the horse for the first time, you can do him a big favor, because this is a step in training that commonly makes a horse claustrophobic. The first surcingle or girth is often thoughtlessly tightened up fast and hard—understandably, this can shock a green horse. It is our challenge and responsibility *never* to give a horse a frightening experience.

The same technique that I use to introduce the surcingle can be used to remediate a horse that is afraid to have the girth tightened.

Note: I think of a horse's stall as his "safe space." It is where he sleeps and eats, and he should be able to relax there. One school of thought believes that the horse shouldn't be disturbed in his stall. However, done carefully and quietly, I find it to be a good place to introduce new things. You should be careful not to use too much pressure when doing so—if your horse is uncomfortable with the introduction to the surcingle or any other piece of equipment and you sense he is becoming overly reactive in his stall, find another small, enclosed area to proceed with your desensitization activities.

- Begin by simply carrying the surcingle over your shoulder when you walk into your horse's stall with his favorite treats in hand. In this first lesson, don't put it on him; brush him, feed him treats, and walk out. If he notices the surcingle or seems bothered by it, repeat the pleasurable input until he forgets or ignores its presence.

- Repeat the preliminary step several times. Then, when he is relaxed and perhaps while you are brushing his back, casually place the surcingle across his back for a moment. Then take it off. Desensitize him step-by-step. Note that repairing the mind of a horse that is already afraid of the surcingle or girth will take far more time than teaching a green horse for the first time in a quiet way.

- Again lay the surcingle across the horse's back. Now rub his belly and apply slight upward pressure there. When he is calm and accepting of the surcingle on his back while you touch and put pressure on his belly, you can finally fasten the surcingle around him. As you begin to tighten it, do it very slowly while distracting him with treats, scratches, and other things he likes. Know your horse, and be prepared to go very easy if he is particularly sensitive or ticklish. Do not tie him; let him move around so that any sense of restriction is relieved.

- Check his ears—are they stiff? Is his eye worried or startled? Is he holding his breath? If yes, do more slow and pleasant work in his safe space. If not, he is probably ready for you to take him to the smallest enclosed arena or pen you have and put the surcingle on there.

- Proceed with an exercise the horse is comfortable with—for example, some basic longeing. Just let him get used to the new pressure as he moves. Start slow and expect him to kick up at his belly or out a bit at the strange feel. Your goal is for him to longe quietly in the surcingle at all three gaits. With slow and patient work for short periods, he will soon take no more notice of the surcingle than he does his halter or cavesson.

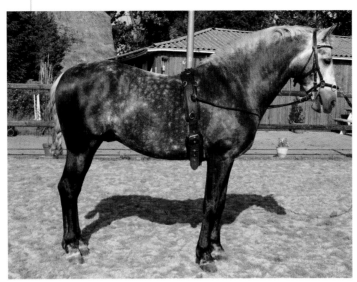

I.I3 Pícaro wears the cavesson, bridle, and surcingle with the side reins clipped to the bit. Although I recommend using the lowest side ring on the surcingle for most horses because this encourages the horse to go "long-and-low," I sometimes work Pícaro on the middle side ring as shown here, which allows his back to stretch without such "forward-and-downward" motion. He is already too heavy on the forehand because of his heavy neck and shoulders.

I.I4 This photo shows the surcingle with full leather side reins correctly secured up and out of the way prior to work. This is how the side reins should be attached when walking to the arena, and when you begin a training session that will involve side reins, this is how they should be secured as you warm the horse up. Never walk from the stable in side reins, with the horse in a fixed position, and it is always best for the horse to warm up properly and loosen his muscles before being fixed in the side reins.

One Pair of Side Reins

I prefer full leather side reins for in-hand work because they encourage the horse to respect the bit and make the horse "softer" (photos 1.13 and 1.14). Another acceptable option is leather side reins with rubber donuts. However, *do not* use elastic side reins. Horses tend to hang on them, and since the elastic reins stretch, they can also "play around" with the contact—sometimes it's there, and sometimes it's not.

INTRODUCING THE SIDE REINS

When the horse is comfortable being longed with the surcingle in all three gaits (see sidebar, p. 23), you can introduce the side reins. Note: a young or green horse should work on the longe for several weeks or even months *without* side reins before you slowly introduce them.

■ As when introducing other new equipment, enter the horse's stall with the side reins draped over your shoulder and some treats in hand. Girth up the surcingle as you usually do prior to work. If the horse is calm, snap the side reins on each side of the surcingle and let them hang there—*they should not be connected to the bit*. Make sure the horse is relaxed.

■ When the horse is comfortable, clip the side reins in a loop on the surcingle as shown in fig. 1.4 so they do not dangle and make your way to the arena. Begin with an exercise the horse is familiar with—do not attempt to attach the reins to the bit until he is relaxed and properly warmed up.

■ In their first fitting, side reins should be adjusted long enough to allow the horse to stretch his neck and head forward and down, while at the same time helping the horse support himself in a balanced stride. To begin, keep the pressure as minimal as possible. Side reins can be snapped to the high, middle, or low rings of the surcingle. The highest rings are used for collection, while the lowest rings are best for the young or green horse doing basic work to allow him to stretch his neck and back. I prefer to clip the side reins on the lowest surcingle ring possible for most of the work I do in-hand. (Note: once the horse is accustomed to side reins you can experiment with fixing them at different positions to see where he works best. But do not force him shorter or higher in the side reins than he seems comfortable.)

■ Begin by asking the horse to perform an exercise he is comfortable with while wearing the side reins—for example, basic longeing. Longe the horse, find the gait and tempo where he seems most comfortable, and just let him move at this speed without asking much more of him. As he begins adjusting to the new balance that he must develop, he may appear to be so preoccupied with his face, head, and neck that he forgets how to walk! Give him time to figure it out without further pressure.

■ Working on side reins is restricting and tiring for horses, so your lessons should be short—no more than 10 to 15 minutes—with frequent rest periods.

Note: Even after your horse is accustomed to work in the side reins, do not use them when you first begin a new exercise. Give yourself, and your horse, time to understand the commands and coordination necessary to perform the lesson correctly before you add the pressure of the side reins.

SIDE REINS: INVALUABLE TOOL OR DANGEROUS DEVICE?

Using side reins as training aids is a controversial subject because they are frequently used incorrectly and can potentially damage the horse physically and psychologically.

Real physical damage can be done to the horse's body. Side reins fixed too short for long periods can compress the front part of the horse's body and put tension in his back. To escape the pressure and discomfort, the horse often pulls his head up and hollows his back, trailing his hindquarters. If his head is bent behind the vertical by force, or if he brings his nose to his chest to evade that force, his weight will be on his forehand and the horse can hardly see where he is going. This is *not* collection and will never lead to the proper strengthening necessary to develop self-carriage.

Real psychological damage can be done to the horse's mind. Some trainers use side reins to dominate the horse psychologically as well as physically. When the horse's head is forced into a fixed position, he is made helpless to a large degree. Horses are demoralized by long periods of longeing in tight side reins. A horse that experiences this type of "training" is likely to become uninterested, frightened, or angry, and will eventually refuse to perform.

However, when used correctly, side reins can help the horse learn to:

- Seek the bit.

- Support his forehand while he is discovering how to balance himself and as his back is strengthened by work in-hand.

- Keep his head straight so he can't twist it to one side, evading work or nipping or biting. (This is most helpful for a handler new to work in-hand, especially if a horse is very young, green, or mouthy.)

- Maintain correct bend to the inside *for a very short period* (accomplished by adjusting the inside side rein one notch shorter than the outside rein).

The ultimate goal is to be able to work with a horse without the use of any artificial "training aids." You will know you have reached this point when you have developed the experience and "feel" to manage a horse without the need for devices.

Whip Etiquette

Several different lengths of whips are traditionally used in work in-hand: the dressage whip, carriage whip, and longe whip.

Whips should be used only as aids to extend our energy. A short, stiff whip (dressage or carriage) allows you to reinforce the aid that your driving hand gives. For example, you can point at the horse with your driving hand to ask him to move away, and if he doesn't heed your aid, a dressage or carriage whip allows you to literally "get closer" to him when you point, or enables you to tap him gently if necessary.

However, because whips can distract horses—the bigger they are, the more frightening they are—and because whips can get in the way, always start with the smallest whip practical for your purposes. When longeing, first try a carriage whip and see how sensitive the horse is to your aids. If he ignores it, try the longe whip, which gives your range of authority more distance. Note: the longe whip will probably make a sensitive horse a little nervous.

In addition to pointing, you can use the whip in other ways to communicate with the horse. You can press the handle of the whip against the horse to enforce lateral movement when you are close to him. You can train the horse to tuck his hindquarters when the whip is touched to his tail, or to stop when you touch his croup. And, if you "swish" the whip in the air behind you, that swishing sounds like an irritated horse's tail that is warning he may bite or kick. I find this swishing sound can get a distracted horse's attention, without inspiring fear.

Sturdy Gloves

I encourage you to always wear gloves to protect your hands, especially your fingers, which may become entangled in loops of reins or lines and be at risk of injury (see photo 2.1, p. 36). I seldom wear them now when working with my more experienced horses, although I still find them indispensable when starting a young, green, or particularly strong horse.

Boots or Protective Footwear

When you work around horses, you are always outsized and quite often outmaneuvered! Limit the chances of injury to your toes and feet by *always* wearing riding or work boots when handling your horses—and certainly when training them in close contact as you are in the lessons in this book.

REMEDIATING FEAR OF THE WHIP

Whips should *never* be used to hit, hurt, or frighten horses. Nevertheless, I often encounter horses—even very young ones—who are frightened of whips. As long as a horse is frightened of the whips you carry, he cannot focus on the lesson at hand. And, a frightened horse is also a dangerous horse.

It is important to start very small when attempting to desensitize a fearful horse to the idea of a whip being in his presence at all, let alone be used in training exercises. As always, use pleasant associations at the same time you are exposing the horse to the thing that triggers him, which is the theory in practice when physicians administer allergy shots to a patient to desensitize him to an allergenic substance.

- To desensitize a horse to the whip, begin by carrying a small stick with you when you go into the horse's stall, or another small "safe space" (see p. 23), while he is eating his grain, or when you groom him or bring him treats.

- Next time, take a larger stick, and the time after that, bring a crop, and then a dressage whip. Let him know with each step that it is just another boring old "thing." Rub it against his neck. Scratch his favorite spot with it. Take the time to build his confidence in you gradually. Do not try to use any kind of whip in training until the horse has lost all fear of the whip in his safe space.

I.15

THE PHILOSOPHY OF TRAINING IN LIGHTNESS

I'd like you to become aware of your habitual interaction with your horse—perhaps horses in general—as you prepare for this program. *Accommodate* your horse's nature, *minimize* your reactions to your horse's negative behavior, and finally, always *cultivate* "lightness" in your handling of him.

Accommodate your horse's sensitive nature by changing training routines in stages to make learning new things less intimidating to him and reduce his stress. For instance, say I have been working my horse in a small, familiar ring where he is comfortable with a certain type of bit, and I decide to progress by moving to a large arena and switch to a new kind of bit. I will begin by working in the large arena with the bit he is used to, and only after he is confident in the large arena will I change to new tack or equipment. Such small considerations develop your horse's confidence that you will never ask more of him than he can do, and on that basis of faith he will try even harder to please you.

Minimize your reaction to your horse's undesirable behavior, and if at all possible, refrain from punishment. Instead, *maximize* your creativity and experiment with positive reinforcement. Use your sense of humor! Ask the misbehaving horse to perform a task at which he excels. For example, when one young stallion I work with gets mouthy, I immediately ask for a few steps of Spanish walk, and he is immediately distracted from fidgeting and becomes busy contemplating his own enormous talent! I can then praise him for a job well done, he is proud and happy, and the result is he will be more cooperative and enthusiastic in the future because he wants to make *me* happy and receive that praise. (Be aware, however, that smart horses may use what they learn from you for their own purposes...teach them the Spanish walk, and they may greet you at the stall door with a salute!)

With the above in mind, you should never tolerate disrespect. It must be remembered that horses let fly a good swift kick or bite when one trespasses another's space—and then usually all is forgotten and they go on eating together peacefully. Rarely is an attitude of threat sustained. The key concept here is to be assertive, *not* aggressive, if and when focus must be encouraged or discipline administered: do it, make your point, and then move on without a grudge...like horses do.

- Cultivate lightness in your own touch to develop an equally light response when you ask a horse to perform for you. Some horses are very sensitive to stimulus and are willing to move with very light aids. Some are not. If your horse falls in the latter category, you may first need to make him more responsive.

    Remember that even the touch of a tiny fly is noticed by a horse, so your task is to use this natural sensitivity to *immediately* get the horse's attention and response. The horse, as a herd animal, naturally responds to *pressure* in the environment around him. The pressure you use can be in the form of your voice, your body language, or your whip (see p. 26). In the lessons ahead, I encourage you to carry a whip, not to be used as punishment, but to point at the horse, tap him lightly, and to otherwise create increased pressure to respond to your commands when he is not immediately willing to do so.

    Always request an action of the horse using the "Rule of Three," which escalates in a way he will soon recognize:

1 Make the first request with subtlety and finesse—think of your ultimate goal, which is to refine your communication with your horse until your aids are invisible.

2 If a second request is required, make the instruction a bit clearer or slightly stronger so the horse understands better.

3 When a third request is required, make your point strongly.

A NOTE ABOUT BOOTS AND LEG WRAPS

I recommend using boots and leg wraps on horses *only* in the case of injury, for the simple reason that they are not necessary on a sound horse. Further, they can actually *create* problems: as an example, the material Neoprene (which is used in many wraps and boots) actually raises the temperature of the leg underneath it by several degrees. Excessive heat is not good for ligaments and tendons.

INCORRECT BODY POSITION
AND WHAT IT CAN TELL YOU

As you begin the exercises in this book, make note of your horse's physical response to your aids. Ask yourself the following questions:

- Does the horse work with his head straight or does he tilt it to one side?

- Does he carry his weight on his own legs, or does he lean on the bit or cavesson?

- Does he bend his head and body to the line of travel on a circle in both directions, or does he carry his head, and lean, to the outside?

- Can he step under himself with his hind legs, bringing his back up and bearing more weight on his hindquarters?

- Does he travel with his head in the air and his hindquarters trailing out behind, leaving him with a hollow back?

It is important to be able to recognize incorrect positions such as those above, because they are problematic for two reasons:

- When the horse is unable to correctly comply with your requests, he cannot optimally benefit from the exercises mentally or physically. You are wasting his time, and your time.

- When he is not performing a certain movement correctly—for instance, if he does not step under himself when you ask for lateral movements, or if he tilts his head instead of carrying it straight—he may simply be resistant or disobedient, or he may be showing you that he is physically uncomfortable. It is important in these cases to have a veterinarian examine the horse for possible stiffness or injury.

Pay attention to what the horse *shows* you, because he cannot *tell* you when something is wrong.

For example: Let's say you'd like the horse to halt in-hand when you stop at his side.

1 For the first request, as you stop walking say "Ha-alt," quietly with the same vocal inflection you plan to use consistently.

2 If you have to ask a second time, repeat "Ha-alt" and this time use body language to reinforce the command—for instance, a "blocking" action such as turning to face him with your body. If he doesn't respect your personal space and your body language, escalate.

3 At the third request, say "Ha-alt" again, take strong contact on the cavesson, and also assertively block his walking forward in some way—such as heading him into a fence—so he is forced to stop.

Challenge yourself to give fewer and progressively lighter aids. In the future when you are in the saddle, your goal will be to give an invisible aid and have the horse perform the required movement until you give another aid to change it. When you achieve this kind of communication, you can sit still on your horse's back—and you'll be together in lightness.

PART II

Longeing and Double-Longeing

INTRODUCTION

Longeing and double-longeing lessons are beneficial whether you are starting work with a new horse, or just want to reevaluate your own horse with fresh eyes and "begin at the beginning" again. As I explained in Part I, in this type of work in-hand, the horse travels in a circle around the trainer at all three basic gaits; obedience, balance, and suppleness on both sides of his body are the goals. In this section, I will first explain how to begin basic longeing with your horse (using one longe line—p. 34), and then progress to double-longeing (using two lines—p. 56).

Some general training recommendations to keep in mind as you begin work on the longe line:

- Work in a calm environment and be serene and gentle when teaching—above all, horses need to be relaxed in order to learn. The more a horse trusts you, the more he is free to focus on you and obey your requests.

- Breathe deeply and regularly while working. When you hold your breath you tense up, thus causing your horse to hold his breath and become tense, too.

- Frequently acknowledge and reward the horse's attempts to understand, obey, and please you with a pat, a treat, or by allowing him to relax by stretching his neck and back in the "forward-and-down" or "long-and-low" posture. At the end of every lesson, reward the horse by inviting him to go long and low, stretching his neck and back as he walks forward and lowers his head. The horse experiences a feeling of relaxation during this stretching exercise because when his head is lowered, his brain makes the endorphins that calm and quiet him. An added bonus is that lowering his head is a submissive gesture—he shows that he trusts you since he is willing to put himself in a vulnerable position in your presence.

Basic Longeing

EVALUATE OBEDIENCE, FLEXIBILITY, AND WEIGHT-CARRYING ABILITY

Goals for This Lesson

- Evaluate the horse's respect for your space
- Determine how flexible he is, and which are his "supple" and "stiff" sides
- Appraise his ability to carry weight on his inside hind leg while on a circle
- Acclimate the horse to the longe line, whip, and moving in both directions in a circle around you

Necessary Equipment

- Working cavesson
- Lead rope
- 25-foot cotton longe line
- Carriage whip and/or longe whip
- A quiet, safe enclosure with corners (Note: although I recommend a round pen for later longe lessons, do not use a round pen for this initial evaluation. A corner provides the horse a space to be free from pressure and think for a minute, or just relax.)

Thoughts before You Begin

Basic longeing—without side reins—helps to loosen and supple the horse, and get him working comfortably on both sides of his body, going in both directions. Many horses are allowed to run and buck on the longe line, and a young horse will undoubtedly take a few wild steps. But, longe work should always be considered part of "formal" schooling and should not be used "to burn off steam" in an uncontrolled manner.

It is a good idea to have an assistant on hand at first to help you teach the horse to stay out on the circle and keep it round (see Step 2, p. 36). The assistant walks a circle between you and the horse, putting "pressure" on him to stay at the end of the longe line. The horse should "seek" the contact with the longeur, and if the longe line is loose, must learn to make the effort necessary to "fill out" the line and find the contact again.

If you don't have an assistant, play a game alternating pressure and release to teach the horse to make a round circle. When he falls to the outside, don't respond by simply pulling because the horse will just pull back (and I'll bet he is stronger than you are!) Plus, you will destroy your light connection with him. Instead, vibrate the longe line to gradually bring him back in. When he cheats too far to the inside, step toward him to "push" him back out with your body language. If that doesn't work, wiggle the longe line up-and-down, creating a "wave" in the line—the motion will help push the horse out away from you. It can also help to work on the longe line in a round pen (although, as noted, not in this first evaluative lesson), as the round shape of the ring encourages the horse to travel in a regular circle and helps him find his own balance more easily. At all times, use your voice to give commands; it helps encourage and focus your horse.

Start and end the lesson by encouraging the horse to lower his head in the long-and-low position, giving him a chance to relax and indicate he trusts you, further creating a good connection for you to work together.

STEP 1

Evaluate the horse's respect for your personal space and his willingness to focus on you.

- With the lead rope attached to the working cavesson (see p. 20), enter the arena with your horse. Test his respect for you, and his focus, by walking, turning, halting, and asking him to yield his space and back up. Observe the level of his willingness to obey you.

Let the horse loose in the ring (leave the cavesson on). Observe his reaction. Does he walk away from you, or head for a corner to escape? How does he respond when you approach him? Is he polite or does he exhibit aggression or rudeness? Does he stay near you? If so, is he interested in you? If not, can you get him to acknowledge you? Taking note of his general attitude and obedience will help you determine what—if any—preliminary groundwork should be done (i.e., voice command for "Whoa," respect for your space) to ensure proceeding with work on the longe line (and later work in-hand) is safe for you both.

STEP 2

Determine how flexible the horse is and which are his "supple" and "stiff" sides.

2.1 Here I am introducing the longe circle to Fernando. My leading hand (left) is positioned forward near the cavesson and my driving hand (right) is holding the excess longe line and the whip so it is pointed backward and toward the ground.

Attach the longe line to the center ring on the cavesson's noseband. Standing on the horse's left, with your right hand nearest the cavesson and your left hand holding the excess line, lead the horse around the arena. Note any hesitation to follow you willingly in this direction. The horse will likely be comfortable because he is used to being led from this side.

Bring the horse into the middle of the arena. Stand at his head, facing him, and pick up your carriage or longe whip (see p. 26 for a discussion of whip etiquette). Switch hand positions so your left hand is nearest the cavesson and your right hand is holding the looped end of the longe line, along with the whip. Your left hand is now the leading hand—it will lead the horse's head in the direction you want him to go (photo 2.1). Your right hand is the driving hand—it will drive the horse's hindquarters in the direction you want him to go with a motion or a touch of the whip.

Using the voice command "Wa-alk," encourage the horse to walk forward with you on a large circle to the left. Face the direction of movement, with your leading hand forward and your driving hand holding the whip so it is pointed backward and toward the ground. Keep an eye on your horse—watch his shoulders, especially, as some horses will barge into your space and walk where they like instead of letting you tell them where to go. If this happens, ask the horse to halt. Wait a moment, then resume forward progress on the circle. Note any unwillingness the horse demonstrates, and any difficulty the horse may appear to have moving in this direction.

● Switch sides, change your hand configuration, and walk your horse on a circle to the right. Make mental note of changes in attitude or way of going as he bends in a circle in this direction.

2.2 Once Fernando is comfortable walking beside me on the circle, I encourage him to walk on a small circle around me by opening my leading shoulder (left) and lifting my leading hand and "pointing" in the direction of travel. I also apply pressure with my driving hand (right) and whip. I try to exude calmness and relaxation with my quiet, still stance.

● Once the horse is comfortable walking beside you in a circle in both directions and you have a general sense of his ability to walk a bending line to the left and to the right, return to your initial position on his left side. Begin this exercise with the horse in the middle of the arena. Combine your voice command to "Wa-alk" with a lift of your leading hand, and create pressure with the driving hand or motion of the whip to encourage him to begin a small circle of 10 to 15 feet in diameter. Slowly feed out the longe line to build up the distance between you and increase the diameter to that of a typical 10-meter working circle—about 30 feet (photo 2.2). Remain as still and relaxed as possible, so your horse, in turn, stays calm.

After several revolutions, decrease the space between you and the horse, gradually shortening the longe line and, using your voice and pressure-and-release on the longe line, ask the horse to halt and turn toward you. Step to his right side, switch your leading and driving hands, and combine your voice command, leading hand and pressure with the driving hand or motion of the whip to ask him to move off. As he moves off on a circle to the right, again methodically increase the diameter to about 10 meters.

Since no horse is perfectly straight, you will probably discover that your horse flexes his head, neck, and body more easily and more correctly on one side or the other. A horse's stiff side can affect his way of going, regardless the direction of travel. For example, if when you longe the horse to the left, he looks and bends slightly to the outside of the circle, with his head and neck almost "counter-bending," then his left side is his supple side and his right side is stiff. The muscles on his right side are not able to stretch and allow bend inward on the circle, and he will undoubtedly "hang" on the longe line, pulling you off the center position. Picture the horse as a banana. Bananas are never straight; they are always curved. The horse's "short, stiff" side is on the inside of the banana's curve, and the "supple" side on the outside of the curve.

Some horses may be stiff on the left and supple on the right, and of course there also varying degrees in between. This step allows you to see how well he can or cannot bend, in which direction he prefers to travel, and helps you determine what work must be done to make him equally balanced and supple on both sides.

STEP 3
Appraise his ability to carry his weight with his inside hind leg on a circle.

To evaluate how well the horse supports his weight by reaching under himself on each side with his hind legs, repeat Step 2 and pay attention to how well his hind legs track on the circle. A horse's supple side is also his "stronger" side, because the horse is working harder with his supple side to carry his weight (also called "compensation" because he is "compensating" with the supple, strong side of his body for what the stiff, weaker side of his body cannot do). When a horse is supple, he can step underneath himself toward the middle of his body to a surprising depth, which helps him curve his body on the circle. When he is not supple, his hind legs can reach underneath only to a shallow degree, and he has trouble curving his body on the circle. Once you have identified his stiff side (see Step 2), you may notice that even

2.3 As I longe him to the right, Fernando carries his weight correctly with his inside hind leg (see arrow), stepping more deeply underneath himself toward the center of his belly.

when the horse is walking straight, he might not reach under himself with his stiff-side hind leg as deeply as his supple-side hind leg. He might even throw that stiff-side hind leg out to the side a little, so it doesn't step in the same track as his foreleg. With this in mind, you can imagine that it will be difficult for him to make a circle correctly on his stiff side.

To illustrate this problem, let us say your horse has a stiff right side and a supple left side (see Step 2). He will undoubtedly find making a left circle more challenging and a right circle easier. When you longe your horse to the *right*, his supple left side will allow him to curve around the circle, but his hindquarters will tend to *fall in* on the circle because his left hind leg (on the outside of the longe circle) is stronger than the stiff-side right hind leg, and propels his weight to the inside of the circle. When longeing to the left, however, his stiff right side will not bend in on the circle and his weak right hind leg will not step under his body deeply enough. This imbalance causes his hindquarters to *drift to the outside*, because his strong left hind leg swings toward the outside of the circle to compensate for his weak right hind leg (which can't support his weight and lands *outside* the track it should correctly fall in). In both directions, you will see that the horse is supporting himself with his supple, strong left hind leg and not properly using his stiff, weak right hind leg (see sidebar and photo 2.3).

When the horse moves *correctly,* he *steps under* his body toward the point of weight with his hind legs. As the horse steps under himself, this allows him to tilt his pelvis under, raise his back, and come off his forehand, a biomechanical relationship that must be functioning before the horse can work toward collection and self-carriage.

When the horse moves *incorrectly,* he *pushes* his weight forward with his hind legs rather than stepping under his body. Although pushing is often easier for the horse (and pushing from behind is necessary for a carriage horse to get a carriage rolling and keep it rolling) it is not correct movement for a ridden horse. Biomechanically, if his hind legs trail behind his body, his back hollows, and his head and neck must come up to compensate for his loss of balance.

Because the hind leg on the horse's stiff side is likely to be pushing rather than stepping under, it is important to understand the difference. This is easy to see on a circle, as when you are longeing. A hind leg that carries always works straight under the horse, or reaches diagonally under the horse. A hind leg that pushes appears to work behind the horse's hindquarters, or the leg is thrown sideways outside the circle.

In this discussion, I am not concerned about where the horse's forelegs are placed on the cir-

cle, although the hind leg should follow the corresponding foreleg. For the moment, think of the forelegs as simply taking the horse in the direction in which he is moving. (Of course, ultimately the forelegs are impacted by the suppleness and strength of the horse's hind legs, because when the hindquarters are stepping under, then the shoulders are free to "open up" and the forelegs are free to reach in front of the horse. Only then can the horse come off his forehand!)

Let us use the same example horse from Step 3, p. 39. He is suppler and stronger on his left side, and stiffer and weaker on his right side (we will call him a "right-bending" horse because he is comparatively contracted on his stiff side as I explained in detail on p. 39). In fig. 2.4 A, this "right-bending" horse is walking on a right circle. Because of this, the bending appears to be easy for the horse, but if you look closely at the hoofprint of his right hind leg, you can see that he is taking shallow steps with that leg instead of reaching under his body and stepping under his point of weight. Even though we must take into consideration the fact that the hindquarters are wider than the chest, the horse's right hind leg is tracking significantly outside his right foreleg, and his right hindquarter is trailing into the inside of his "circle."

In fig. 2.4 B, our right-bending horse is now trying to walk on a circle to the left. Clearly, the horse
is counterbending because he is so stiff on his
right side he cannot bend to the inside of the circle. But look closely at his right hind leg. If you ask
the "unsupple" horse to bend to the inside (left in
this case), his right hind leg will swing to the outside even more because his right-side muscles don't
have the length to allow him to pick his right hind
leg up and place it under his body. Therefore, the
right hind leg is trailing to the outside of the circle.

In fig. 2.4 C, a right-bending horse is walking on
a circle to the right, but even though his right hind
leg is weaker and stiffer than his left hind leg, at this
moment he is using it correctly. This is the goal of
in-hand work—he needs to train his weak leg; otherwise, he will stay stiff and crooked.

In fig. 2.4 D, the right-bending horse is again
walking on a left circle. Compare this illustration to
fig. 2.4 B. The horse's bend has improved (it is now
only slightly right), but as before his stronger left
hind leg is propelling his hindquarters to the outside of the circle. The horse must learn to use his
right hind leg more actively to keep his hindquarters from falling out on the circle. (You can help him
straighten his body by using side reins, as I discuss
on p. 25.)

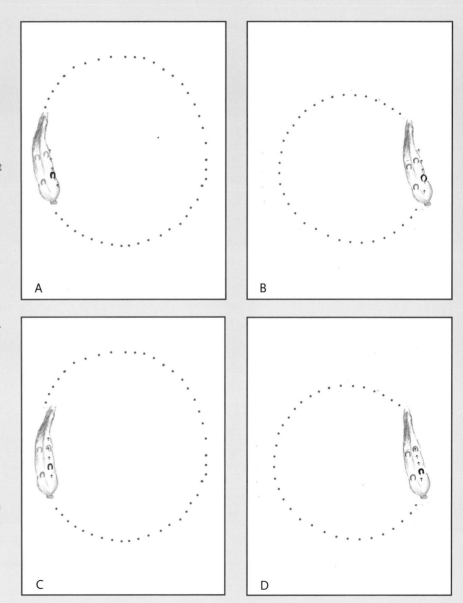

Troubleshooting

WHEN THE HORSE...

...is uncooperative, or exhibits behavior such as pinned ears, biting, invading your space, or refusing to yield his space at your request.

Try this:

Improve his basic ground manners before attempting more challenging work.

WHEN THE HORSE...

...falls in on the circle.

Try this:

Wiggle the longe line into a "wave-like" motion, point at his shoulder with the whip, or touch him on the shoulder if he comes too close to you. You can also ask for an assistant's aid to reestablish the circle before moving on (see p. 35).

WHEN THE HORSE...

...looks to the outside of the circle, "throwing" his inside shoulder toward you.

Try this:

"Point" the finger of your driving hand or the whip at his inside shoulder, encouraging him to move his shoulder away from you and bring his nose more toward you. At the same time invite his head inside by vibrating the longe line but do so carefully so the horse doesn't overreact to a too-strong aid and fall in with his forehand.

WHEN THE HORSE...

... is not willing to bend along the circle line and seems to have trouble flexing.

Try this:

Walk beside him on the circle as at the beginning of Step 2. Place the back of your driving hand on the horse's lower neck, and gently bend his nose toward the inside with your leading hand to ask him to flex his neck. Then release, walk a few strides, and repeat. Do this exercise for very short periods at first, gradually building up the length of time you hold the flexion until the horse is able to bend himself and stay bent. Work on both sides of the horse—you will find that the exercise also "loosens" his hips, which allows the horse to "swing" with his spine. So this is a very good training for a supple back!

WHEN THE HORSE...

... has difficulty bringing his inside hind leg underneath him on the circle.

Try this:

Walk beside him on a small circle. Keep the pace of the walk slow so it is easier for the horse. The faster the pace, the more the horse will push; you don't want him to push—he needs to "carry his weight" by reaching under himself. On a circle to the left, you want the inside (left) hind leg to step further under the body. The moment when the horse's outside front leg is going to lift, touch the inside hind leg with the whip to trigger and encourage a more active stride forward. In addition to teaching the horse to step toward the point of weight, you also ask him to bring his inside hip forward. By doing so, he is swinging his spine—a step toward the goal of suppleness!

Make only tiny, gentle corrections to keep him bending on the circle or you will pull his nose toward you and his hindquarters will swing out. Since this is a suppling exercise, he needs to bend his neck and body along the arc of the circle.

Lesson 2
WALK, HALT, TROT, CANTER

Goals for This Lesson

■ Develop rhythm, balance, and power
■ Teach the three basic gaits and halt using verbal commands and body language

Necessary Equipment

- Working cavesson
- 25-foot cotton longe line
- Carriage whip and/or longe whip
- Arena or round pen

Thoughts before You Begin

Begin your first few longe lessons by walking your horse in-hand for several circles, before then letting him out slowly so he is walking *around* you in a circle of 25 to 30 feet (approximately 10 meters) in diameter (see Lesson 1, Step 2). In the beginning, the horse should follow a circle almost as large as the width of the arena, as large circles allow him to focus on you without feeling too much pressure to flex and bend. Additionally, if he has a particularly difficult side (he is very stiff or has trouble stepping under with his inside hind leg) or is claustrophobic when he moves between you and the arena fence or wall, the large circle gives you enough space to relieve his tension.

Always repeat each step in both directions. The goal is to be able to work your horse equally on both sides. However, your initial attempts to stretch and supple your horse may require that he has extra time working on his stiff side. In this case, begin the lesson longeing on your horse's stiff side, change to the supple side, and then finish the lesson on the stiff side, so he is worked twice on the stiff side and once on the supple side. As his stiff side becomes supple, you may find the "old" supple side needs more attention, and so you must start the process again, reversing it if necessary. Because you are actively influencing the development of your horse, you should consider this continual remodeling a sign of good training.

As mentioned in Lesson 1, it is best to teach your horse to halt on command *before* you get to this lesson. A confirmed "Whoa" will help you control him on a large longe circle and at various speeds.

STEP 1

Walk and halt on a large circle.

• For this first step, start from the left side—regardless which side is your horse's stiff side—because the horse is used to being handled from the left and it helps to begin with the familiar. Hold the longe line in your left hand and the neatly folded excess line along with the whip in your right. Aim your belly button toward the middle of his body and point the direction (in this case, left) with your leading arm (fig. 2.5).

• To ask him to move forward on the circle, continue to show the horse the direction of movement desired with your leading hand (left); point your belly button toward his hindquarters, which has a driving effect; "open" your left shoulder "like a door" so he is free to move; lift your driving hand holding the whip, say "Wa-alk," and then lower it (fig. 2.6). This lifting action of the driving hand puts pressure on the horse to move forward. If he doesn't respond to your first request, remember to use the Rule of Three (see p. 29):

• For your second request, indicate the direction of travel with the leading hand, and point the whip at your horse's hindquarters with your driving hand. Then, stand with your arms wide and held at shoulder height, lowering your leading arm so you don't block his go-forward energy as you raise your driving hand and repeat the command "Wa-alk." Be aware of what you are doing with your arms. When you raise both arms at once, you "chase" him away from you.

• If you need to ask a third time, add to the above cues by "swishing" the air with the whip. This sound will "wake the horse up" and cause him to move off. However, only do this as a last resort as it may make some horses nervous and tense. Overcome your own tension by standing with both feet on the ground, breathing deeply, and relaxing—and then your horse is more likely to stay relaxed, too.

2.5 The beginning position for basic longeing: Hold the longe line in your leading hand, which points in the direction of travel, and the neatly folded excess line along with the whip in your driving hand, which motivates the hindquarters. Aim your belly button toward the middle of the horse's body.

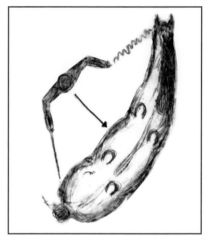

2.6 Ask the horse to move forward on the circle by showing him intended the direction of movement with your leading hand. In addition, point your belly button toward his hindquarters, "open" your leading shoulder, lift your driving hand holding the whip, and say "Wa-alk."

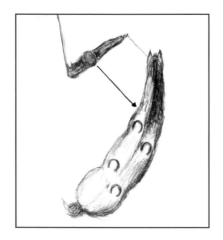

2.7 To halt the horse on the longe line, lower your driving arm (pointing the whip to the side and behind you), raise your leading arm, and step toward the horse's shoulder to "block" his way as you say "Ha-alt" in a low voice.

At first, keep the horse close to you, but then gradually ask him to move outward onto a larger circle. Avoid pulling on his head or neck to force him to flex inward. Instead, vibrate the line to "invite" him to turn his head himself.

To halt: lower your driving arm, raise your leading arm, say "Ha-alt" in a low, slow voice, and step toward his shoulder to, in effect, "close the door" and "block" his way (fig. 2.7 and photo 2.8).

Change direction while your horse is at the halt, moving to his right side and pointing with your leading hand in the new direction (right). Send him on as you did when going to the left. At this point in training, *don't try to change directions while your horse is moving*. If he becomes confused or frightened, he will run off, which is counter to the confidence and consequent "lightness" you are hoping to instill.

Alternate four or five walk circles on each side.

STEP 2
Trot on a large circle.

Begin in the center of the circle with the horse moving round you at the walk. Raise your driving arm to pressure him to move forward, keeping your leading arm low, and in an energetic voice give the verbal command, "Trot!" If necessary, use the whip together with the physical aids you used when you asked the horse to walk on the circle in Step 1 (photo 2.9). Start with the horse close to you, but gradually increase the size of the circle as soon as you feel comfortable. Never trot for long on a small circle as it strains joints and ligaments in undeveloped bodies.

Watch the horse's movement carefully for the "size of stride" that suits him, and which will therefore help him develop rhythm, balance, and power. Control the tempo of the trot by talking

2.8 Even with the longe line loose and only light contact on the cavesson, Fernando halts upon my command. Note my raised leading arm (left), "closed" left shoulder, and the driving hand and whip pointed away from his hindquarters.

2.9 Fernando picks up the trot on a small longe circle (note: I will increase the size of the circle as soon as I feel he is comfortable with this new command. Trotting on a small circle for extended lengths of time is not recommended for young, undeveloped horses). My leading (left) shoulder is "open," I have a light contact with the cavesson, and my right hand (holding the whip) points toward his hindquarters and helps drive him forward.

to the horse. You want to encourage a regular, even rhythm that relaxes him and allows him to bend comfortably along the arc of the circle.

- To slow from the trot to a walk, say, "Wa-alk," raise your leading hand and turn your left shoulder toward the horse so your body faces his hindquarters, "blocking" his forward movement. Don't forget to lower your driving arm.

- Alternate direction, circling four or five times on each side.

STEP 3
Change direction on vocal command.

- From a walk, ask the horse to halt on the circle.

- Say the word you always will use to indicate he should change direction (for example, "Hup!").

- Pull lightly on the cavesson to begin turning him to the inside of the circle, toward you, and switch the longe line into your new leading hand, which should now point in the opposite direction, and the whip into your new driving hand.

- As the horse crosses the circle in front of you and moves off in the new direction, gently "wave" the longe line to send him back out onto a larger circle. If need be, take a step toward him, and use your new driving hand and whip to "push" him out.

- Repeat in both directions.

STEP 4

Canter on a large circle.

● Caution: do not proceed to this step until you have worked with your horse on the longe at walk, trot, and halt for several weeks. The canter energizes horses, encouraging bucking and other misbehavior in both the young and those that just don't want to focus on the work at hand. The well-behaved horse must demonstrate partnership with his handler by staying calm and cooperative at all times, with no rough or random behavior. I never allow a horse to act out—from the moment I put a halter on him to the moment I return him to his stall or pasture at the end of the day. Therefore, it is best to be comfortable in your ability to control the horse at all gaits, and to be sure you have confirmed vocal commands and the halt, before attempting the canter.

● Ask for your first canter transition from a steady, rhythmical trot on a fairly large circle (keep the horse close enough so you can control him, but allow enough room for the increased stride and speed). In an energetic voice, use the verbal command, "Can-ter!" Lower your driving shoulder and at the same time move your driving arm toward his hindquarters, as if you are "chasing" him with your body a little. Most horses respond within the first few times you ask. If not, use the Rule of Three (see p. 29).

● You want the horse to canter in a controlled manner, maintaining his focus on you, but the excitement of working at a higher speed may cause him to take off a little too fast. To slow him down, use your voice to calm him. If you need a stronger aid, move your body toward his shoulders, lower your driving arm, raise your leading arm, and "block" his way with your presence— just enough to get his attention, but not enough to cause him to break into a trot. The goal is for the horse to canter on the longe line with a steady, controlled rhythm and tempo, just as you had established at the trot.

● Work four or five circles in each direction.

Practice upward and downward transitions.

Now you can combine the three gaits and halt in transition work. Mix it up, frequently changing gait to keep the exercise interesting and gymnasticize the horse. Do note, however, that before attempting the big upward transitions, such as walk-to-canter or halt-to-canter, the horse must respond precisely to your aids. Remember to work with your voice, body, and arms and hands as I've illustrated in the preceding steps, because your body language is your means of control over the horse. In particular, always be aware of what your arms are doing. Control your breathing and stay oriented to the middle of your horse's body, even when moving fore and aft to alternately slow the horse or drive him forward.

Troubleshooting

WHEN THE HORSE...

...doesn't respond to your aids (voice and body language) to move forward.

Try this:

"Swish" your whip in the air to get his attention and give him energy.

WHEN THE HORSE...

...will not halt.

Try this:

Continue giving the horse the verbal command to "Ha-alt," shorten the longe line in small stages, and establish a steady contact to regain control. Position yourself toward the front of his body, so he doesn't feel that you are chasing him, and use *half-halts* on the cavesson to get his attention. Do this by alternately "squeezing" and "releasing" the longe line. If he is still unresponsive, shorten the longe line further and step toward his head or shoulder to "block" him.

WHEN THE HORSE...

...trots too fast or "runs away."

Try this:

Shorten the longe line a little, hand by hand, very quietly, to make the circle smaller and regain control. Lower your driving hand and raise your leading hand a bit. The moment the horse slows, praise him lavishly.

Lesson 3
LONGEING IN SIDE REINS

Goals for This Lesson

■ Help the horse develop strength, "roundness," and rhythm

■ Teach the horse to take a soft contact on the bit without overly tiring him

■ Teach the horse obedience to the outside rein (which will help when you ride him later)

■ Encourage the horse to compress his body for short periods and learn to use his back

■ Bring the horse into a better position by lightening his forehand slightly

Necessary Equipment

■ Working cavesson fitted under the bridle with full cheek snaffle (see p. 20)

■ 25-foot cotton longe line

■ Surcingle (see p. 21)

■ Side reins (see p. 24)

■ Carriage whip and/or dressage whip

■ A quiet, safe arena or roundpen

Thoughts before You Begin

Always begin each lesson by warming up the horse in the cavesson and bridle *without* the side reins. When you first attach the side reins, they should initially be adjusted long enough so he can stretch his head toward the ground and not feel "fixed" and claustrophobic. Make large circles—the width of the arena or 25 to 30 feet in diameter; smaller circles put more pressure on his joints as he's struggling to rebalance his body in the side reins. Keep him calm—patience and time are your two best friends.

Teach the horse to longe in side reins at the walk, trot, and canter over time; do not try this in one day. Trotting and cantering in side reins is more difficult to perform correctly in the beginning, because as his speed increases, the horse is likely to swing his hindquarters to the outside of the circle. You want a balanced movement where the horse is "carrying himself," so he needs to travel in a controlled manner. Again, give him time to become accustomed to the new position of his head and neck, and the different way his body must move to compensate. In addition, take care to end each lesson before the horse gets sore or frustrated. You want him to come willingly to his exercises.

Only when the horse is calm working in the longer side reins at all three gaits and halt should you gradually shorten them (see more about this process on p. 25). Carefully watching him for signs of discomfort or nervousness. Your goal is to ultimately use the side reins at a length where the horse can move freely with his head held a little in front of the vertical. Remember, the purpose of side reins is to help him compress his body a little bit, and support him while he uses different muscles and becomes balanced.

After he is well adjusted to the shorter side reins—comfortable and obedient longeing in both directions, in all three gaits, and in upward and downward transitions—they can be adjusted one notch shorter on the inside to help the horse bend around the circle. This should be done only for short periods of time—for example, five minutes on each side.

Caution: *Do not* longe your horse with the longe line attached to the bit, for two important reasons. The horse's soft mouth is very sensitive and longeing on the bit is one way to begin "desensitizing" it, with all the pulling that longeing can involve. Also, when the longe line is attached to the bit, the horse is more likely to twist his head and evade work. Although some professional trainers are qualified to longe a horse on the bit for remedial or other special reasons and find it an effective technique, for in-hand training, I strongly discourage the practice. Instead, always attach the longe line to the center ring of the working cavesson. (I should note, however, that since the double-longeing exercise—see p. 56—is the precursor to long-lining, we will be attaching the longe lines to the bit at that time.)

STEP 1

Walk and halt on the longe in side reins.

- As in prior longeing lessons, begin your new lesson on the horse's left side, holding the longe line in your leading left hand and the whip in your driving right hand. Aim your belly button toward the middle of your horse's body, and drive him forward with your voice and body language (see p. 45). At first work close to him and gradually ask him to move outward onto a larger circle.

- After the horse is walking and relaxed on the longe circle *without* the side reins, ask him to halt. Remember, to stop the horse on the circle, move toward his shoulder, face him, and raise your leading hand to "block" him while saying "Ha-alt" or "Whoa." Approach him and now clip the side reins to the bit. Note: If this is his one of his first lessons in side reins, they should be adjusted long enough that he can stretch his head forward and down (see preliminary discussion on p. 25).

- Again move the horse out on the longe circle, and ask him to walk and halt on the circle.

- Change direction and work with the horse on his right side (photos 2.10 A–C). Work four or five circles in each direction.

2.10 A–C As Fernando walks on a circle to the right in the side reins, I ask him to halt by raising my leading hand (right), "closing" my right shoulder, and lowering my driving hand (left). As Fernando had been schooled in side reins prior to this lesson, they are adjusted so that he can move comfortably with his head a little in front of the vertical, and I have them one notch shorter on the inside than the outside.

STEP 2

Trot on the longe in side reins.

- Once the horse is comfortable at the walk and halt, in both directions, ask him to trot in the usual way by giving the verbal command "Trot!" and lowering your leading hand while raising your driving hand. The horse may find it difficult to trot in the side reins until he learns to make steady contact with the bit. The resulting uneven rhythm is often made worse by the horse's lack of fitness and balance. In time, the horse's rhythm will improve. When he does trot at the desired tempo and rhythm (even just by luck!), reward him by allowing him to walk and praise him with your voice.

- Change direction. Work four or five circles each way.

STEP 3

Canter on the longe in side reins.

- Even if the horse is working well in the side reins at the walk and trot, I recommend detaching them and warming the horse up at the canter with his head free for a short time. When he canters in a controlled, balanced manner in both directions, bring him to a halt and reattach the side reins (remember, use a longer length if early in his training in side reins).

- When you first ask him to canter in side reins, your horse may take off a bit fast as he figures out his new balance and grows accustomed to making contact with the bit. To slow him, use the technique described on p. 46.

- Work four or five circles in each direction.

STEP 4

Practice changing direction and upward and downward transitions.

● As you did in your basic longe training (see p. 46), combine the three gaits, halt, and change of direction upon command as you practice making transitions with the horse in side reins (note: when planning to change direction upon command, be sure the side reins are both adjusted to the same length). Wait until he responds precisely to your aids before you try "big" upward or downward transitions (such as canter-to-halt). Remember to work with your body, arms, and voice; control your breath, and stay oriented to the middle of your horse's body.

Troubleshooting

WHEN THE HORSE...

...is not working in a controlled, focused way on the large circle due to the addition of and distraction offered by the side reins.

Try this:

Temporarily bring him in onto a slightly smaller circle where you can control him better. However, take care to not work for too long on a small circle; short, successful lessons performed often are best.

WHEN THE HORSE...

...tends to move with a lot of weight on his forehand due to big shoulders and a big neck (as with many Baroque horses and stallions).

Try this:

Work with slightly shorter side reins than you use normally. However, watch the horse carefully for signs of discomfort or tension and keep each lesson to 10 to 15 minutes, at the most.

WHEN THE HORSE...

...bends inward too much when circling on his stiff side, and counterbends to the outside when circling on his supple side.

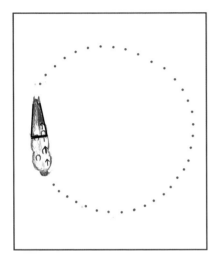

2.11 This drawing shows how with the help of side reins, the "right-bending" horse (see sidebar on p. 40 for further discussion) has been straightened in his body, and his hind legs are tracking correctly behind his forelegs.

Try this:

Longe him in side reins (they should be adjusted to be the same length). Invite his nose toward the inside with the longe line, and when he bends his head and neck toward you, his hind leg will come better under his body instead of trailing toward the inside of the circle (fig. 2.11). The straightness offered by the side reins allows you to work on training a specific hind leg (see further discussion on p. 40).

Double-Longeing

Lesson 1
INTRODUCTION TO THE DOUBLE LONGE LINES

Goals for This Lesson
- Familiarize the horse with the sensation of two longe lines coming into contact with his body
- Introduce him to the feel of two points of contact on either side of the cavesson
- Prepare him for more demanding exercises and "pressure" exerted by the lines on either side of his body

Equipment Needed
- Working cavesson
- Bridle and full-cheek snaffle
- Surcingle
- Side reins
- Two, 25-foot cotton longe lines

■ Quiet "safe space" (such as the horse's stall—see p. 23) and an enclosed arena

Thoughts before You Begin

When double-longeing, you use *two* longe lines attached to the *side* rings of the working caves-son, instead of one attached to the center ring. As in basic longeing, you stand in the middle of a circle while the horse travels around you, only now you are holding two lines—one on each side of the horse's body. The sensation of the contact from the longe line(s) is likely to be unfamiliar to your horse, and some horses are more sensitive on their sides, back, hindquarters, and under the tail, so take the time you need for your horse to become comfortable. You do not want him to lose confidence when he first feels this new "pressure" from the longe lines.

STEP 1
Introduce the double longe lines in the horse's "safe space."

● Tack up in an enclosed space where the horse feels comfortable and safe, such as his stall. Begin with the surcingle, cavesson, and bridle. Then run the two longe lines through the lowest rings on the surcingle and attach them to the side rings on the cavesson. Move the lines around, sliding them along the horse's sides, over his back, around his rump, and down his hind legs. Let the horse get used to the feel of the lines all over him, as well as contact on both sides of the cavesson.

● When the horse remains calm with the two longe lines moving around and over him, attach the side reins to the lowest surcingle rings that are available to use, and to the bit. If there is enough room for both the longe lines and the side reins on the lowest rings, clip them there (be certain, however, the longe lines do not obstruct the side rein clip or buckle). Use the lowest rings possible for the side reins so your horse has the opportunity to stretch his back to the maximum and hold his head and neck in the long-and-low position. In the case of the longe lines, the low surcingle rings almost guarantee the outside longe line will stay behind the horse's hindquarters as you work him, and not slide up and under his tail or over his back, causing you to lose control of the horse's offside.

● Reacquaint the horse with this tack and equipment several times—on and off—for a few days in a row, until you are sure that he is comfortable in it.

● When you are ready to work the horse in the double longe lines, lead him from his "safe space" or stall to the arena with the nearside longe line attached to the cavesson. The offside longe line should be coiled and clipped to the middle ring on the offside of the surcingle. The side reins can be clipped to the surcingle, but do not attach them to the bit until your horse is warmed up and ready to begin his lesson in the ring. You may just want to carry them to the arena separately. Always arrange your double-longe equipment this way prior to your workout.

Lesson 2
DOUBLE-LONGEING ON THE CIRCLE AND FIGURE EIGHT

Goals for This Lesson
■ Control the horse's bend and counter-bend
■ Stretch, relax, compress, and collect the horse
■ "Shape" and support the horse's hindquarters with the outside line, preventing him shifting too much weight to his inside shoulder

Equipment Needed
■ Working cavesson

- Bridle and full-cheek snaffle
- Surcingle
- Side reins
- Two, 25-foot cotton longe lines
- Carriage whip and/or dressage whip (Note: I find a longe whip heavy and awkward to handle when changing direction)
- Arena or round pen

Thoughts before You Begin

Double-longeing is an invaluable technique to help control the horse's head and hindquarters with the inside longe line and the drape of the outside longe line around the horse's hind end. This, in turn, allows you to achieve some collection. In addition, when you ask the horse to bend with the two lines, you can—in effect—"shape him" with them, flexing his head inside the circle while supporting him with the outside line, and even working on counter-bend by shortening the outside line a little more to supple him (see photos 2.10 A–C). Here the horse's supple and stiff sides will again likely come into play (see p. 36), and you will find the second longe line on the outside of his body invaluable in preventing him from "falling out."

When double-longeing, the inside longe line can exert a great deal of "drag" on the horse's forehand. If you and the horse are not balanced, as individuals and as a pair, you can create a centrifugal effect—"pulling" his head toward you causes him to automatically throw his hindquarters out. For this reason, it is *very important* that the horse is relaxed and stable in all the basic longeing exercises, with and without side reins, before you attempt to double-longe him (see pp. 34–56).

Three distinct stages comprise the process of teaching a horse to double-longe, and they concern the horse's graduation from one configuration of training equipment to another. Within each stage, work the horse in circles in both directions. *Do not try to master all three stages on one day.* If you have problems at this point in the process, it is probably because you are pushing the horse too fast.

Caution: Before you begin this exercise, ensure that the horse halts on command. You are now working with two separate lines, and if the horse makes a fast turn, it is rather too easy to become tangled if he does not immediately and consistently obey your halt command. Also, if you are working with a circle smaller than 20 to 25 feet and have extra line in your hands, keep it looped neatly. This is critical because if your loops are messy and the horse leaves the circle suddenly, your fingers, hands, or body can get caught in the lines.

STEP 1

Stage One: With both longe lines "loose" (not run through the surcingle), and without side reins, longe the horse on a circle with the outside line draped over his back. Halt, walk, trot.

- Start on the horse's left side with one longe line attached to the nearside ring on the cavesson. Uncoil the offside line, which should be clipped to one of the right middle surcingle rings, *not* the horse's head (see Lesson 1, p. 58), and bring it over the horse's back to his left side.

- Assume your usual longeing position, in the middle of the circle the horse will travel. The inside line (in this case, the left) should be in your leading hand (left), and the outside line (clipped to the right-side surcingle ring and draped over the horse's back) should be in your driving hand (right).

- Accustom the horse to being longed from the left side of the cavesson with the outside longe line draped over his back (photo 2.12). Always work with one line in each hand. *Do not* hold both lines in one hand.

- In early lessons, allow the horse as much freedom of movement as possible so you can win his trust. As you did when initially working with him in his stall (see p. 57), make sure he is relaxed with your moving the longe lines along his sides, around his hindquarters, and under his tail. The horse will likely tuck his rump when he feels the line behind his hindquarters.

He should be comfortable at walk and halt with this new configuration before you attempt the trot. Work him in both directions.

2.12 Stage One of the introduction to double-longeing: Fernando trots with good forward impulsion with the inside longe line "loose" (not run through the nearside surcingle ring) and the outside long line clipped to the offside surcingle ring and draped over his back.

● Stay as light as possible with the line contact. At first when you are unaccustomed to managing two longe lines, it will be a strong temptation to pull too hard on either—or both—the forehand or the hindquarters of the horse.

STEP 2

Stage Two: With the inside line "loose" (not run through the surcingle), the outside line clipped to the cavesson (or bit), and run through the lowest offside surcingle ring and around the horse's hindquarters (under his tail), and the side reins clipped to the lowest surcingle rings and the bit, longe the horse on a circle. Halt, walk, trot.

● Start on the horse's left side with the inside longe line clipped to the nearside cavesson ring (or the bit), but *not* run through the nearside surcingle ring. Run the outside longe line through the offside surcingle ring and clip it to the offside ring of the cavesson. Attach the side reins to the lowest surcingle rings and to the bit (photo 2.13). Remember, when you use side reins, you "fix" a horse in place, so *never* make them tight. At their shortest setting, the horse should be able to put his nose out just beyond the vertical (see further discussion p. 25).

● Accustom the horse to the outside longe line draped around his hindquarters and under his tail, and to the contact offered by the side reins, at the halt, walk, and trot in both directions.

STEP 3

Stage Three: With both lines through the surcingle rings and attached to the cavesson or the bit, and without side reins, longe the horse on a circle. Walk, halt, trot.

• When you reach this stage, remove the side reins. Run the inside longe line through the surcingle ring to the nearside cavesson ring. The outside line should still be attached to the offside cavesson ring and run through the offside surcingle ring (fig. 2.14).

• Alternately halt, walk, and trot in both directions until the horse is comfortable. Remember, now that the inside longe line is run through the nearside surcingle ring, you have a powerful leverage on the inside of the horse.

• Next attach both longe lines to the bit rather than the cavesson rings (photo 2.15). Do not rush to this step—make sure you are comfortable handling the double longe lines and the horse is obedient and relaxed at all gaits and halt. This can be very hard on his mouth if you are not careful.

• Again practice transitions in the halt, walk, and trot, and work in both directions.

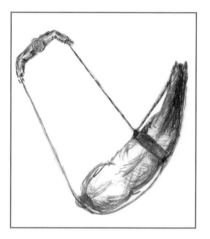

2.14 Several progressive steps lead to the scenario depicted in this illustration (see Stages One and Two, pp. 60 and 62): the most effective position you can use to double-longe the horse. Assume your usual longeing position, in the middle of the circle with your leading hand handling the inside longe line, and your driving hand handling the outside longe line. The inside longe line is run through the nearside middle surcingle ring and attached to the cavesson or the bit, and the outside longe line—also attached to the cavesson or bit—is run through the offside middle surcingle ring and round the horse's hindquarters. You can now exert both a powerful leverage on the inside of the longe circle and control counter-bend and flexion on the outside of the longe circle.

2.15 I double-longe Fernando at the trot in Stage Three of the introduction to double-longeing: both longe lines are attached to the bit and run through the surcingle rings on either side. I am maintaining a consistent but light contact with both my leading and driving hands, as you can see by set and flexion of Fernando's head and neck and the gentle, even "loop" of the lines between us.

STEP 4

Stage Three: With the same configuration of tack and equipment, make a figure eight and change direction.

2.16 As we near "X" in the middle of the arena on a circle to the left, I begin to heighten contact with the right longe line (which was the "outside" line, but will now—in the figure eight pattern—become the "inside" line). Note how Fernando's bend has changed from the inside of the circle (left) to slightly right. He is ready for me to fall in behind him as we change rein and begin a circle to the right, completing the figure eight.

● The figure eight requires good timing and definitely takes practice—you should be very proud when you and your horse do it smoothly! You cannot work in a small arena or round pen for this step as you need room to cross the diagonal (in addition, the horse must learn to work in larger spaces and not depend on the "psychological support" a small enclosed area provides). Be aware that a larger arena may give him a sense of freedom, so watch his eyes and ears. Make sure the horse is focusing on you and his work before proceeding, or the exercise won't be successful.

● At one end of the arena, ask the horse to make several circles around you to the left at a walk. After several times round, as he crosses the center "X" of the arena, pull gently on the outside longe line to straighten the horse (photo 2.16). Fall behind him momentarily.

● As you and the horse cross the center "X," shorten the ""new"" inside line in your right hand, and let the new outside line become longer in your left hand. Move to the right side of the horse, running the new outside line behind the horse's hindquarters as you take up your position in the center of a new longe circle. Make a circle to the right at the end of the arena, and then repeat the process, again changing rein at "X" and completing a figure eight (fig. 2.17).

● Be thoughtful and patient during this exercise because there is a big shift in the pressure of the reins and a significant change in your body position when you ask him to circle at one end of the arena then cross the center and circle again in the opposite direction.

Troubleshooting

WHEN THE HORSE...

...doesn't accept the longe line behind his hindquarters.

Try this:

Return to his "safe space" where he felt more secure, and repeat the work you did to desensitize him to the equipment before moving to the arena.

WHEN THE HORSE...

...starts to pull you around the arena.

Try this:

Don't ignore this bad habit for a moment! Immediately put him in side reins—if he is not already in them—or shorten them a notch if he is, to provide the contact he is seeking. The horse will accept the bit when he has *consistent* contact; human hands can be tense, busy, and disturbing to the horse, especially when you are learning to master a new skill, such as managing two 25-foot-long longe lines, plus a whip! It can also help to find a smaller area to work in until you have more control. If necessary, you can create a temporary enclosure *within* your arena with stakes and plastic tape that will break (should a horse run through it). I sometimes do this in my larger fields in Holland.

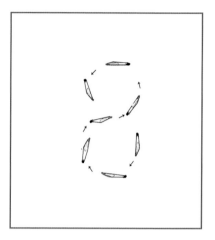

2.17 The figure eight pattern when using the double longe lines. Note: The handler should return to his position in the mddle of the circle after changing rein—this is not depicted here.

PART III

Long-Lining

INTRODUCTION

When long-lining—as mentioned before, a natural progression from double-longeing (see p. 56)—you walk *behind* the horse at the end of two longe lines, actually "driving" him as if he were pulling a carriage. You can walk, trot, halt, change rein across the diagonal, and reverse direction at the end of the track. You need to have good control over the horse for this work because you are a fair distance behind him where he cannot see you, and your only means of communication is through the bridle and your voice. This exercise is a real test of your horse's sensitivity and obedience. Here, his willingness and ability to pay attention to your voice will pay off!

At first, long-lining may look difficult and seem overwhelming when compared to the more common practice of longeing, but remember: millions of horses have pulled carriages, wagons, and other conveyances throughout history, and they have always been accompanied by handlers who somehow managed to drive two, four, even eight horses at one time. I have no doubt you can learn to long-line one horse!

As you begin this lesson, keep in mind that because the horse is at such a distance from you—when performed correctly about 25 feet (see photo 3.2, p. 73)—it is most disruptive when the horse attempts to turn back toward you. It is also unsafe as he may get his feet caught in the lines and trip. Consequently, I highly recommend you *do not* feed him treats when he is working in long lines, and use only your voice as praise. I always say, "Keep the horse rewarded," but even I can forget myself and go too far, spoiling my horse. Recently I was working Pícaro in long reins (see p. 168) at the counter-canter, and he did it so well that I cried out, "Oh, what a good boy!" He immediately leaped in the air, turned 180 degrees in the reins, and rushed back to me for a cookie.

As in all in-hand lessons, you are teaching obedience when long-lining, and it is of particular importance when the horse is working at such a distance from you. In the end, not all horses can be safely long-lined. Or, you may have to wait until a young horse is more seasoned or a naughty horse better behaved before attempting the lessons in this section. Know both your horse's limits, and your own.

Lesson 1
WALK, HALT, TROT, REIN-BACK, CHANGE REIN ACROSS THE DIAGONAL, AND REVERSE DIRECTION

Goals for This Lesson

■ Prepare the horse for work in long reins (see p. 143) and/or driving
■ Teach the horse to travel in a straight line and make basic school figures
■ Introduce the horse to steering and communication via rein aids
■ Give the handler a feel for proper use of the reins—when to pick them up, when to release them, and how to achieve a deft touch

Necessary Equipment

■ Working cavesson
■ Bridle with a full-cheek snaffle
■ Surcingle
■ Side reins
■ Two, 25-foot cotton longe lines
■ Carriage whip and/or dressage whip (Note: I find a longe whip heavy and awkward to handle when changing direction in the long lines)
■ Arena or enclosed workspace at least 50 x 50 feet

Thoughts before You Begin

Be sure you have mastered basic longeing and double-longeing (pp. 33–65) before attempting this lesson. The aids and movements involved in longeing exercises provide both you and your horse the necessary background for successful long-lining work. Even so, you may need to break the complex steps in this lesson into "bite-size" pieces.

Whether you use the bridle or cavesson in this lesson depends on your horse's sensitivity and obedience. If the horse is just started in training and has never worn a snaffle, you can begin with the cavesson, which makes your commands clear to a horse that is responsive to it. On the other hand, some horses will "run through" the cavesson—ignoring your directions. Since safety is *always* most important (don't let yourself be dragged!), stronger, more opinionated horses might be better off learning this lesson in the snaffle. You'll see in the photos on the following pages that I attach the reins to the snaffle or the cavesson with the same horse, depending on the day and exercise.

The use of side reins while working on the long lines teaches the horse continuous contact with the handler through the bit and the function of the outside ("outside" the bend) rein. The outside rein is the most important rein in riding because it limits the bend so you can control the straightness of the horse's body.

STEP 1

Prepare for the long-lining exercise by double-longeing in a circle and making a figure eight.

● Warm up with a double-longeing session to reacquaint the horse with the distance between you and the feeling of the longe lines along his body and around his hindquarters (see p. 60). Start on his left side beginning with one longe line attached to the cavesson or bit, then both, and after he is working comfortably and calmly, practice the figure eight (see p. 64).

STEP 2

Walk straight between the long lines on the long track.

● Guide the horse to the long side of the arena and gradually fall back behind him (photo 3.1).

● Watch carefully if your horse is prone to kicking.

Stay on the long track so the fence or wall supports him on one side as you gradually fall back to the ideal distance behind him (photo 3.2). If you work in the middle of the arena, the horse may drift. When the horse gets off-track, quietly correct him with the outside line. It is important to be consistent and continue to communicate your leadership from the increased distance. Remember, he cannot see you so he may feel insecure.

3.1 The long lines are attached to the cavesson and run through the middle side rings on the surcingle. The side reins are adjusted loosely to give Ufaro room to become accustomed to this new lesson. As we approach the fence line, I adjust my position from that of double-longeing, gradually falling in behind him.

STEP 3

Halt on the long track.

To halt the horse in the long lines as you walk behind him on the straight track, close your hands on the lines (as you would on the reins if you were riding), and say "Ha-alt" in the same voice you used when longeing. Maintain contact on the cavesson or bit until the horse slows down and stops. When he responds correctly, be sure you do not "throw the reins away" (drop contact completely) as the horse will become unsure and you may lose both his attention and your control. Use your usual voice aids to praise him for a job well done and ask him to walk on again.

Practice transitions between walk and halt along the long side. You should be confident that you have established the "brakes" before moving on to Step 4.

STEP 4

Rein-back on the long track.

Rein-back can be a challenge when using long lines since you are at a distance behind the horse, but as always, any lesson is an exercise in obedience. Begin at the halt on the long track with the fence or wall on one side to support the horse. Keep soft contact with the horse and close your hands, while at the same time "vibrating" both hands and giving your verbal command for your horse to back up. (This can be any word, such as "Ba-ack," but use it consistently from now on whenever requesting the rein-back, both in-hand and in the saddle.) Maintain the vibrating pressure until the horse yields and takes a step back. Immediately relax the aid when he responds, even if it's only one step in the beginning, and praise him.

Remember, since your horse cannot see you, his only guidance comes from your hands, your voice, and the long lines along his sides and hindquarters. He may be very unsure of what you are asking and even stop—if so, vibrate the lines on either side of him to encourage him to back up in response to the pressure you are putting on the cavesson or bit. If he still does not back up, you may have to increase the pressure considerably—even lean back on the lines, literally putting your weight on them in slight increments until the horse responds with a step. As soon as he does, release the pressure while maintaining contact, and praise him.

3.2 In this photo, I am falling back to the ideal distance for long lining—about 25 feet. Note that before we advanced to this stage, I changed my tack configuration: the long lines are now attached to the snaffle, above the clips for the side reins (be sure they do not interfere with each other). My hands are light, steady, and even and as is ideal when riding, there is an unbroken line from my elbows to the horse's mouth.

A horse performing a correct rein-back lifts his hooves and steps backward with diagonal pairs of legs evenly, rhythmically, and in a straight line. If he drags or scrapes his feet, try just a step or two of rein-back, and then make a quick transition forward to the walk to energize him. It is important to note that the horse's back has to be strong to lift his feet correctly in rein-back, so ask for a little at first, and build on the exercise as he gains in condition.

STEP 5

Prepare for trotting in the long lines by double-longeing in a circle out to the track.

● Before you ask your horse to trot on the long side of the arena between the long lines, it is best to give him an idea of what you want *without* providing him the opportunity to run off. This can be accomplished by first double-longeing him in a circle in the center of the arena at the trot (see p. 62).

(see p. 62)

● As he circles, gradually move toward the long side of the arena until he eventually meets the track and the arena fence or wall. At this point, quietly straighten him from a bending line to a straight line and fall in behind him on the track. If he gains too much speed, immediately return to your double-longeing position and make circles back toward the middle of the arena to regain control. Then, again attempt to work your way to the outside track and trotting on a straight line.

● Once your horse moves forward steadily in the trot on straight and bending lines with you at the ideal long-line distance behind him, experiment with downward trot-walk and walk-halt transitions. In addition, practice picking up the trot from the walk on the long track (photo 3.3).

3.3 Ufaro picks up a lovely, balanced, controlled trot on the rail. Although he cannot see me in my long-lining position behind him, you can tell by his ears and concentrated expression that he is listening to my aids carefully. I have a little more tension on the right-hand line (toward the outside of the arena) to help keep him straight on the long track.

STEP 6

Change rein across the diagonal and reverse direction.

- To change rein across the diagonal when tracking to the left, as you are turning the corner from the short side of the arena to the long side, take up a little pressure on the inside (left) line and look in the direction you want to turn. Lighten your feel on the outside (right) line but maintain contact with your horse's mouth. As you cross the arena on the diagonal, stay right behind him with equal weight on both reins or he will lose his straightness. When he nears the long side of the arena again (now facing the opposite direction), lay the right long line (now the inside) against his right hindquarter to straighten him in the new direction along the track. The fence or wall on his left will help him "turn to" the right rein.

- To reverse direction at any location in the arena, turn and make a "teardrop" shape, doubling back on your previous line of travel. For example, as you walk along the track on the left rein, when you come to the point where you wish to change direction, increase pressure on the left line and "give" with the right and begin a circle, but then after a quarter- to a half-turn, head straight back to the long track that you just left, now going in the opposite direction (fig. 3.4). As with changing rein across the diagonal, when the horse nears the fence or wall, lay the right line against his right hindquarter to straight him along the track. Again, the fence or wall on his left will help him turn to the right rein.

Troubleshooting

WHEN THE HORSE...

...does not consistently obey the halt command.

Try this:

It is important at all times that a horse knows that "Halt" means *halt,* wherever you are and whatever you are doing. When first beginning work on the long lines, horses often feel "free" because you are at quite a distance behind them. However, a horse that doesn't know and

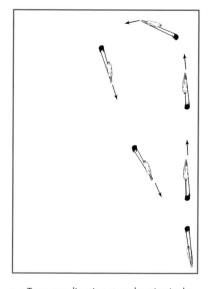

3.4 To reverse direction at any location in the arena, turn and make a "teardrop" shape, doubling back on your previous line of travel. This illustration shows what it would look like when on the left rein. As you come to the point where you wish to change direction, increase pressure on the left line, "give" with the right, and turn a quarter- to a half-circle, heading straight back to the long track that you just left, now going in the opposite direction.

respect "Halt" at this stage of the game is missing an integral piece of his education, and you don't have real control. When he walks on even after you've asked him to halt, try giving *half-halts* to get his attention. Half-halts are a valuable tool from here on out—you will use them both in-hand and in the saddle. The half-halt is a combination of aids that asks the horse for his attention without stopping him. For both work in-hand and riding, I squeeze my hands on the reins, bring my upper body back, and indicate with a verbal command what I would like the horse to do (for instance, "Trot!" or "Canter!") all at the same time. Think of the halt-halt as a "half-hold."

When long-lining and asking for the halt, try first for the half-halt by alternately "squeezing" and releasing the lines at the same time. The moment you feel him "come back to you," close your hands and say "Ha-alt." If he stands still, even just for a few moments, immediately praise him with your voice and allow him to walk on as further reward.

WHEN THE HORSE...

... "pulls" you around the arena, speeding up or running away.

Try this:

Don't ignore this bad habit for a moment! Immediately bring the horse around into a circle so you are double-longeing him (as in Step 5, p. 74) and continue to double-longe until you have regained control. If you continue to experience this problem when you return to the straight-away, put your horse in side reins if he is not already in them, or shorten them slightly if he is. It will also help to work in a smaller area where you have more "psychological control" for the time being (see my recommendations on p. 18).

PART IV

Work in Short Reins

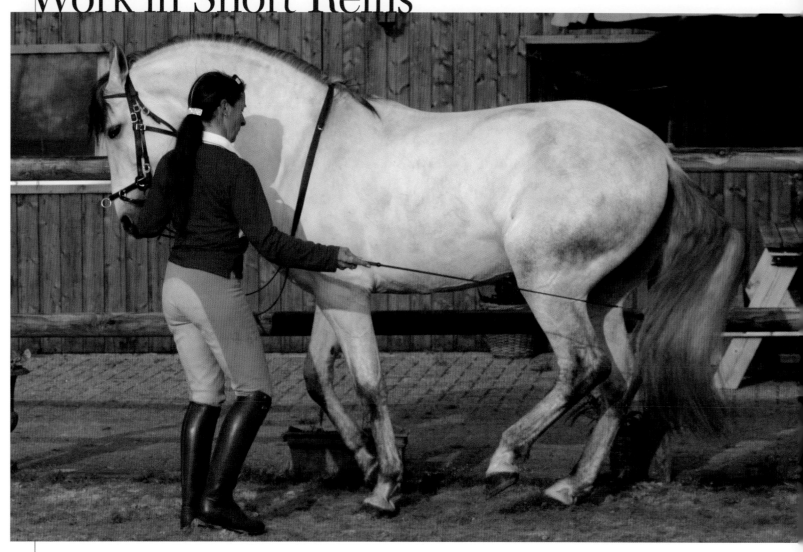

INTRODUCTION

Now you begin formal lateral work!

By this time you and your horse have become attuned to each other with your longeing, double-longeing, and long-lining work. Your horse should be cooperative—listening to your voice and responding correctly to requests for direction from the long lines. He should display no fear of you or the whip.

Caution: If your horse has a tendency toward biting, striking with his front legs, or falling to the inside and "throwing" his shoulder into your space, remember that you become vulnerable when you work as close to him as you must using the short reins. And, when you are working with an excitable or unmannerly horse—or a stallion that may take your presence on the ground as a challenge—working him in the short reins may not be a safe option. *Know your horse,* and be honest with yourself regarding your ability to handle him before beginning these lessons.

Several rather complex concepts come into play as you begin work in short reins. These include *lateral movement, speed*, and *space.*

Defining Basic Lateral Positions

The great benefits of work in-hand are derived from the various combinations of moving the horse forward and sideways at the same time while asking the horse for some degree of bending. This combination supples and strengthens the horse at the same time. On the following pages, I briefly discuss the different lateral positions that the horse and handler use relative to the parameters of the arena you are working in.

As mentioned in Part I (p. 6), I use the term "track" frequently in lateral work, a word that has multiple meanings. I will touch on them briefly again here.

When the horse's body position is closest to the fence or wall of the arena, "on the rail," as some might say, he is on the track. Next to the track, immediately toward the inside of the arena, is the inside track. Imagine you and a friend are riding around the arena, chatting and cooling your horses out after a lesson. If you are riding next to the fence, and she is riding next to you on the inside, you are on the track and she is on the inside track.

The horse's body may stay on one track, or span both, depending on the exercise. When he is straight, he is traveling on a single track, when he spans both the track and the inside track, he is performing a two-track movement.

We also use the term tracks to refer to how many legs we can see if we are standing directly in front of the horse as he advances toward us—this can be two, three, or four tracks, depending on the exercise. When a horse is walking straight toward you with his hind feet directly following his front, you can only see two legs—he is on two tracks. When a horse is performing lateral movements—moving sideways and forward at the same time—in some movements you can see three legs (three tracks) and in other movements four legs (four tracks). Using shoulder-in (p. 101) as an example: the horse's hindquarters are positioned on the track and his forehand on the inside track, and shoulder-in is most often performed on three tracks as is required in dressage competition. It can also be performed in the classical manner on four tracks. (To compare, see figs. 4.4 A & B, p. 82.)

This may seem confusing now, but as you work through the lessons in this section, the above concepts will become clearer. In addition, the drawings that follow present a "bird's eye" view of the basic lateral movements used in-hand. You can easily see how the horse is positioned as compared to the arena fence or wall; whether he is bending toward or away from the direction of movement (depicted by an arrow); the degree of bending; and whether he is on two, three, or four tracks.

POSITION	DESCRIPTION

4.1 Straight

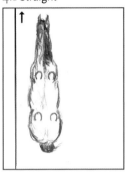

The horse's body is parallel to the line of travel (and in this case, the arena fence), and his weight placed equally on each leg. He faces the direction of movement, there is no longitudinal bend (though he is slightly flexed—see p. 13), and he moves on two tracks with the left hind foot tracking into or just in front of the prints left by his left front foot, and right hind doing the same on the right side.

POSITION	DESCRIPTION

4.2 Straight but bending

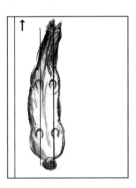

The horse's body is parallel to the arena fence, and he faces the direction of movement on two tracks, but now we've incorporated a slight bend to the inside of the arena. This inside bend actually helps his hind feet to travel the path of the forehand as shown in fig. 4.1. Because the horse's forehand is narrower than his hindquarters, the hind feet naturally step wider than the front. To straighten a horse, you must gain control of the hindquarters and create engagement that allows the hind feet to step closer to each other and therefore in the actual tracks of the front—as in this mild exercise.

POSITION	DESCRIPTION
4.3 Yield to the "leg" (p. 96) 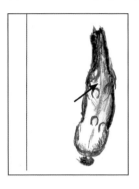	The yield to the "leg" exercise (in-hand, the role of your "leg" is played by your body position, or driving hand or finger) can be performed anywhere in the arena; here it is shown as a diagonal movement away from the arena fence or wall. The horse is slightly bent toward the rail, so he is looking away from the direction of movement (see arrow). He should be on four tracks and his inside front and hind legs cross in front of his outside legs (remember, *inside* means *inside the bend*). Because he must step deeply under his body with his inside hind leg while reaching out with the diagonal foreleg, this is an excellent gymnastic exercise.

POSITION	DESCRIPTION
4.4 Three-track and four-track shoulder-in (p. 101) 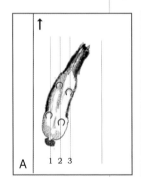 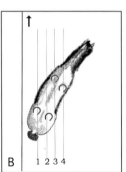	As I mentioned earlier, the three-track shoulder-in is more commonly practiced, as it is the one required in competitive dressage (A). The four-track shoulder-in, in the style of la Guérinière, is more lateral and demands more strength and athletic ability from the horse (B). In A, the horse's legs are moving on three tracks: the left hind leg on one, the right hind leg and left front leg on another, and the right front leg on a third. He is bent toward the inside of the arena, away from the direction of movement (down the rail), with his forehand brought in off the track at about a 30-degree angle to the arena fence or wall. This exercise helps strengthen the horse's *inside* hind leg as he brings it under his body toward the point of weight.

POSITION	DESCRIPTION

4.5 Shoulder-out (p. 101)

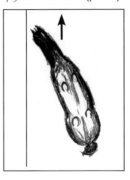

In the shoulder-out, the horse begins on the inside track and his forehand is brought toward the fence or wall (onto the track). The degree of bend is the same as the three-track shoulder-in, which is shoulder-out's mirror image. Shoulder-out is a three-track exercise with the horse bent away from the direction of movement (down the rail). This exercise helps strengthen the horse's *inside* ("inside" the bend) hind leg as he brings it under his body toward the point of weight.

POSITION	DESCRIPTION

4.6 Half-pass (p. 112)

Compare the half-pass with the yield to the "leg" (p. 82). The direction of travel (diagonal, away from the arena fence or wall) is the same, but the horse is bent *toward* rather than *away* from it. His body remains parallel to the rail as his forehand slightly leads and the outside legs cross in front of the inside legs on two tracks. The half-pass is a great suppling and strengthening exercise.

POSITION	DESCRIPTION
4.7 Renvers or haunches-out (p. 118)	The renvers is an excellent suppling exercise and has great gymnastic value. In the renvers, the horse's hindquarters remain on the track and the forehand is brought in onto the inside track at about a 30-degree angle to the rail. The horse is bent in the direction of movement (down the rail) and he is moving on three tracks. However, a flexible horse can walk on four tracks so you see all four legs. Although you should "start small" and begin with the renvers on three tracks, for optimum flexibility, your ultimate goal for your horse would be, in time, to school him in the renvers exercise on four tracks.

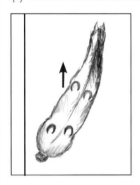

POSITION	DESCRIPTION
4.8 Travers or haunches-in (p. 122)	In the travers, the horse's forehand remains on the track and his hindquarters are on the inside track at about a 30-degree angle to the rail. The horse is bent in the direction of movement (down the rail) and he is moving on three tracks when you begin schooling in travers. However, as with renvers, to develop optimum flexibility, after the travers on three tracks is mastered you may school the horse in travers on four tracks.

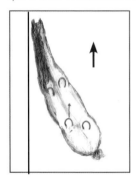

Speed

Speed is how much ground is covered in a unit of time. It can be changed by altering the gait, the horse's length of stride, or the gait's tempo (the rate of repetition of strides per minute). As you begin work with short reins, watch your horse's speed, as well as your own. Never run beside your horse; when you hurry and run, he will hurry and run too, and he can run much faster! Or, he might become nervous if he feels your hurrying expresses a state of tension (and he might be guessing right).

Always try to walk the same speed that your horse is walking. Skip a step or two to keep up with him now and then if necessary. If you need to slow him down, in combination with your other aids, slow your steps and breathe deeply and quietly. He will feel you relaxing and respond in kind.

Although we always begin training in-hand exercises at the walk, and will do so now in the short reins, as the horse becomes more experienced and obedient, it is a further challenge (and so beautiful!) to work at a collected trot and even a very collected canter. Consider working in these gaits an advanced step to all the exercises in this section.

Space

Remember that horses can feel claustrophobic and often perceive enclosed spaces as "pressure." When you are working your horse closely in-hand, such as in the short reins, always be aware of your body language and how you use your eyes. Horses "read" our body language and expression in the same way we read theirs, and you don't want to be perceived as a threat. Even a sustained human stare may cause a horse unease because it instinctively reminds him of the unnerving "predatory gaze" his ancestors encountered in the wild. Something as ordinary as being placed (i.e. "trapped") between you and the fence or wall of the arena during an exercise can be equally troubling to a sensitive animal.

On the other hand, some horses may find your presence and/or a sense of containment comforting. For example, I currently have a horse in training that tends to be nervous when I walk beside him on a circle in the middle of the arena, and as soon as we return to the track where he is positioned between me and the fence, he begins calming down. In his case, I believe he is seeking a "safe" space and he feels "supported" by the physical "corral" formed by my body and the fence.

Lesson 1
WALK, HALT, REIN-BACK, AND TROT ON THE RAIL

Goals for This Lesson

- Develop the horse's attentiveness and precise responsiveness to your aids
- Increase acceptance of your "polite domination" of his space
- Introduce schooling in a space between you and the arena fence or wall (Note: resistance to this kind of containment is mainly a problem with stallions, extremely sensitive or young horses, or those with bad manners)
- Establish rein "contact" via the cavesson and bit

Necessary Equipment

- Working cavesson
- Bridle with full-cheek snaffle
- Surcingle
- Side reins (optional)
- One set short reins (attached to the side rings of the cavesson in Stage Two)
- Cotton longe or lead line (attached to the center ring of the cavesson—note: this is necessary in Stage One and a good safety precaution during all initial lessons in the short reins)
- Dressage whip
- Rectangular arena

Thoughts before You Begin

On short reins, you work close to the horse at his head, neck, shoulder, or side, usually along the arena fence or wall (unless you are performing yield or half-pass exercises in which you move across the diagonal). It may take you some time to become comfortable with your new position in relationship with the horse.

Perform all the exercises in this chapter in both directions, with you positioned on both sides of the horse. As with earlier lessons, I recommend that you begin each new one on the left side of the horse, but once he is familiar with it, start with his *stiff* side, change to his *supple* side, and end the lesson working the stiff side again (see p. 9). This method enables the horse to supple his stiff side more effectively. (In the process, you may find that you, too, have a stiff and a supple side!)

There are two distinct stages in teaching a horse to work in short reins and they concern the horse's graduation from one configuration of training equipment to another. Within each stage, work the horse in both directions. *Do not try to master both stages in one day.* If you have problems at this point in the process, it is probably because you are pushing the horse too fast.

STEP 1

Stage One: Walk on the rail with the longe or lead line.

For this lesson, a cotton longe or lead line should be clipped to the center ring of the cavesson. You are not using the short reins yet. Position yourself at the horse's left shoulder facing the horse—this is the correct position for handling a horse in short reins. Your leading hand holds the longe or lead line close to the horse's head (see photo 4.10A, p. 89), and your driving hand holds the excess longe or lead line and whip. Hold the dressage whip handle up and shaft down except when using it. When needed, rotate the whip so the handle is down and the shaft is up, and flex your wrist so the shaft of the whip is held horizontal, parallel to the horse's body (photo 4.9). This can take some practice! I find that in this proximity to the horse, holding the whip along his side—even without touching him—can encourage him to move or straighten him. When a stronger aid is needed, press your driving hand against the girth area, and when necessary, press or tap the whip against the horse's side.

4.9 The dressage whip in "active" mode: when my hand is held normally with my thumb on top, the end of the whip handle points toward the ground and the shaft points up. I then flex my wrist and rotate the whip so the shaft of the whip is held horizontal, parallel to the horse's body, as shown here.

Walk in a circle to the left, rotating your hips slightly to the left to lessen the amount your legs need to cross in order to move forward. Gradually move the horse from the circle to the long side of the arena. Make sure the horse bends correctly as you move on the arc of the circle and doesn't evade your aids (photos 4.10 A & B).

Straighten the horse on the track, positioned between you and the fence or wall of the arena, and walk beside him for three or four steps. Then, leave the rail to begin another circle on the left rein. Again return to the track, and this time straighten him for several more steps along the fence. Continue this pattern until you are walking straight down the entire long side of the arena with the horse calmly respecting your new position near his head.

4.10 A & B In A, Fernando bends slightly to the inside, from poll to tail, as he walks in a circle with me beside him in the position appropriate for work in short reins. In B you can see him evading my aids to bend his body on the arc of the circle—he has "broken" his neck toward me while striding straight ahead.

STEP 2

Stage One: Halt on the rail with the longe or lead line.

● When the horse works well in the walk along the track, introduce the halt. After several straight steps, raise your leading hand, say "Ha-alt" in same voice you've used in lessons prior and turn your left shoulder toward the horse so that you are at a 90-degree angle to his shoulder. Move the end of the whip gently on to the top of his hindquarters as you tell him to halt, to give him extra support and to introduce an additional halt cue (photo 4.11). In the future, when the halt is required for other exercises, you only have to put the whip there and he will respond. However,

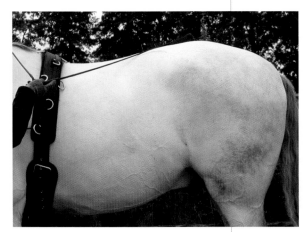

4.11 When you ask for the halt from the short reins position, place the end of the whip gently on to the top of your horse's hindquarters. This will become an additional—and useful—halt cue as you proceed with work in-hand.

the first time you ask he probably won't stop! Remember the Rule of Three (see p. 29), and repeat the command, now vibrating the line on the cavesson, and increasing the pressure with your body as needed until he finally halts. Praise him.

● Once you have successfully completed a few halts along the track, check to see if your horse is standing straight and square at the halt. He should not be falling in toward you or out away from you—his body should be parallel to the arena fence or wall and his front and hind legs should be relatively even and each bearing an equal amount of weight. (It is desirable to instill this habit now so he stands straight and square later under saddle.) This is a good test of your own position, too: If you are too far forward (near his head), your presence and the consequent pressure he feels may cause him to swing his hindquarters out in the halt. When this happens, fall back a bit toward his shoulder to create a more neutral posture. If you are too far back (near his side), he may turn inside with his forehand when you halt. Correct this by moving forward a bit. You can also position your driving hand and whip alongside him, not necessarily touching him, to help "support" him and keep him straight.

● When your horse halts willingly, straight and square, on the rail, ask for the halt again, but now try to reduce your body language. For instance, decrease the degree of angle where you block him with your body from 90 degrees to 45 degrees. Then, see if he will respond when you remain facing him and simply flex your shoulders back a bit. Lessen the amount you use your voice and how much you vibrate the line. Then try to just move the whip to the top of his hindquarters to see if he responds. Soon you will be able to halt your horse with only the slightest of aids.

STEP 3
Stage One: Rein-back on the rail with the longe or lead line.

● As described earlier in this book, in a correct rein-back, the horse lifts his feet and steps backward with the diagonal pairs rhythmically and evenly. His ability to do this well depends on his physical condition and strength. Practicing the rein-back happens to be an excellent way to improve physical condition and increase back strength because in order to back up, the horse lowers his hindquarters, balances his weight over them, and raises his back. Incorporate the rein-back in your work along the rail. Begin at the walk on the left rein and ask for the halt. Turn 90 degrees so your left shoulder is at your horse's head and your body faces his hindquarters. Using the voice command you taught him on the long lines (see p. 73), ask him to "Back." Your leading hand should have loose contact on the longe or lead line—vibrate it to encourage the horse to back away. Escalate the pressure as necessary. Keep the horse straight by holding your driving hand and whip up alongside him.

- When he has offered you one rein-back step with each foot, reward him by letting him go "forward and down" and remember to praise him liberally. Horses don't like to back up because they can't see where they are going, and backing up is also a sign of submission. Note: with a young or underdeveloped horse, ask for only a step or two at first and build his strength over time.

- Make it easier for the horse to understand what you are asking by requesting the rein-back at the same place on the rail for a while. However, once he has the hang of it, be sure to back him at different places in the arena. When a horse learns to perform a movement in one particular spot only, he will likely have trouble managing it elsewhere.

STEP 4
Stage One: Trot on the rail with the longe or lead line.

- Before you begin this exercise, make sure your horse's "brakes" work! He should be willing and comfortable doing walk-to-halt and halt-to-walk transitions in-hand.

- Begin at the walk on the left rein on the perimeter of the arena. When you reach the long side, give your vocal command for the trot. If he doesn't respond, increase the pressure with your driving hand and whip. Be prepared to have to walk quite quickly and with long strides to keep up with him.

- Allow just a few steps of trot and then transition back to walk with your voice command, a turn of your body toward the side of the horse, and vibration on the line. Increase the number of trot steps gradually. When the horse goes too fast, circle toward the inside of the arena to get control of his speed, then bring him straight along the track again. When he is gentle and obedient, ask him to reduce his speed a little by turning your left shoulder toward him and blocking his forward drive. This begins a bit of collection.

- When he moves forward steadily in the trot, experiment with trot-walk and walk-halt transitions.

STEP 5

Stage Two: Repeat Steps 1 through 4 in the short reins.

- Once you and your horse have mastered Steps 1 through 4 using the working cavesson and the longe or lead line, attach one set of short reins to the side rings of the cavesson. If you wish, keep the longe or lead line attached to the center ring for safety. If you are using side reins, clip them to the cavesson rings.

- Stand at the horse's left shoulder, facing him. Hold the cavesson rein nearest you in your leading hand, close to the horse's head where you have the most control (the leading hand should also hold the longe or lead line if you are using it—photos 4.12 A & B). Bring the outside rein over the horse's withers and hold it in your driving hand near the horse's shoulder. The driving hand also holds the whip (see p. 87 for tips on whip use). Be conscious of your own body. Do not let your driving hand float too high on the horse's back, but keep it at the girth line, near spur height. Hold your leading hand and rein near the horse's mouth (although watch the

4.12 A & B The correct position for work in-hand in short reins begins with you standing at the horse's shoulder, facing him. Hold the cavesson rein on your side of the horse in your leading hand, close to the horse's head where you have the most control (the leading hand should also hold the longe or lead line if you are using it, as shown here). The rein on the opposite side of the horse should come over his back and into your driving hand, which also holds the whip and any excess longe or lead line.

"mouthy" horse that likes to nip). If you hold this hand up too high, it may go numb. After all, this work is all about feeling!

● Ask the horse to walk along the rail on the left rein using your voice, body, and your driving hand, which applies pressure in the same place on the horse's side—the girth area—that you would apply pressure with your leg. You should be accustomed to moving beside the horse in this position by now, so you can concentrate on developing the horse's responses to the reins. Use the inside rein (left) to invite the horse to come to the inside, keeping contact with the out-side rein (right) against his neck to support his movement. Use the right rein to ask him to turn away from you, again keeping contact with the left rein against his neck to support him. Use both reins with equal pressure to keep the horse straight. In other words, keep contact with the horse's "mouth" with both hands in the same way you would when you ride.

● Ask the horse to halt on the rail. An important advantage between earlier in-hand work where you schooled the horse on the longe (when you "hold" the horse with only one hand and must rely on your voice and body position to communicate with him) and in short reins (when you hold the horse with two reins fixed either to a cavesson or snaffle bit) is that you can squeeze and/or vibrate both hands to aid the horse to stop.

● Ask the horse for the rein-back on the rail. From the halt, continue vibrating the reins to ask him for a step backward. Since you are next to the horse at shoulder position you can "pull" a little with both reins if necessary. You will find it is easier to keep the horse straight during the rein-back with two reins.

● When your horse is comfortable walking, halting, and backing-up in the short reins, ask for the trot along the rail. Use the same aids that you have used for trot work in earlier lessons.

4.13 Tanguillo wears a cavesson, bridle, and two pairs of short reins, all adjusted correctly for work in-hand.

● Only once the horse is light and responsive in the cavesson and short reins should you add the bridle, bit, and second pair of short reins (photo 4.13). (Note: when working with a particularly difficult horse, you can use the bridle and short reins earlier in Stage Two to help keep control and ensure obedience and precision.) Repeat Steps 1 through 4, introducing the rein action on the bit and using the reins on the cavesson to reinforce your aids.

● Once you begin using the short reins in this way, you are a step nearer to riding the horse. For now, use a combination of verbal and physical commands, but plan to eliminate the former. The ideal aid is just the slightest vibration of the rein; and of course, this is one of the ways to make the horse light and responsive.

Troubleshooting

WHEN THE HORSE...

...repeatedly ignores your halt command, even when you turn your shoulder toward him.

Try this:

Remember the Rule of Three (see p. 29): for a second request, turn at a 90-degree angle to his shoulder, raise your leading hand, say "Ha-alt" again, and *step in front* of his shoulder, facing his hindquarters. If needed, your third request can be walking him in a circle, aiming him toward the arena fence or wall, and using it as a barrier as you say "Ha-alt." Each time, give a little vibration on the line or reins, like the feeling you get from your vibrating cell phone. Do this a few more times so your horse gets the idea.

WHEN THE HORSE...

... will not accept working between you and the fence.

Try this:

Don't insist. Go back to working him in-hand on the circle in the center of the arena, and each time around return to the track, ask your horse for three steps along the rail, halt for a moment, and ask him to look at the fence. Then circle again. Repeat this process until the horse is comfortable.

WHEN THE HORSE...

...does not back up with your first request.

Try this:

Say "Back," vibrate the line or reins, and then pull back and maintain the pressure until he responds. For your third request, say "Back," vibrate the line or reins, pull back, and also tap your horse's chest with your fingers, or, if you need to, touch or press the whip to his chest.

Apply pressure until he responds. One step is enough; your first goal is only one.

WHEN THE HORSE...

...falls in with his hindquarters.

Try this:

Use the arena fence or wall to "support" and straighten him on the outside, and hold the whip horizontally, parallel to his body and pointed at his hindquarters to support him on the inside. When the horse is not paying attention, give him a tap on the hip with the whip. If necessary, bring his forehand to the inside track to help "push" his hindquarters toward the rail.

WHEN THE HORSE...

...tries to bolt or go too fast.

Try this:

Young horses in particular will bolt if they become frustrated with the new lesson and "pressure" they feel when working in the short reins. Correct sporadic or spontaneous forward movement by immediately guiding the horse in a circle to help you regain control. However, do not spin the horse around you, or allow him to whirl around his forehand, as this can damage his legs.

Lesson 2
YIELD TO THE "LEG"

Therapeutic Benefits

- Stretches the muscles on the outside of the horse's body ("outside" the slight bend)
- Strengthens the inside hind leg as it steps underneath the horse to support his weight

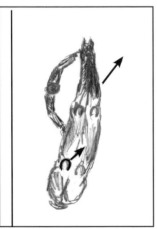

4.14 Therapeutic benefits of yielding to the "leg" include stretching the outside muscles of the body and strengthening the inside hind leg.

Goals for This Lesson

- Introduce lateral movement
- Teach the horse to be obedient to the pressure of the handler and the leg of the rider
- Help the horse learn to use his inside hind leg without strain or overreaching

Necessary Equipment

- Working cavesson
- Bridle with full-cheek snaffle
- Surcingle
- Side reins (optional)
- Short reins (one or two pairs depending on horse's stage of training)
- Cotton longe or lead line (optional)
- Dressage whip
- Rectangular arena

Thoughts before You Begin

Work in-hand in the short reins requires obedience and responsiveness. The yield to the "leg" is a psychologically powerful lesson to teach a horse. It is a lateral movement that you use not only to supple the horse, but also to teach him respect for your presence next to his body, or your hand pressing against him. Teaching the yield from the ground prepares him to obey your leg when you are mounted. And, it is the building block for the shoulder-in exercise that follows (see p. 101). Since the horse naturally relies upon his hindquarters (his engine) for impulsion to quickly get him out of danger, when you control their movement, you essentially control the horse.

As you begin this lesson, think about how being "pushed" and "pulled" affects a horse psychologically. Horses don't pull on each other like we pull on them with halters or bridles. They put pressure on and push each other with variations of body language, such as pinning their ears, giving nasty looks, tossing their head, running at each other, snapping at the air, and if all else fails, connecting physically with bites and kicks. When you put pressure on a horse with your expression, body position, hand, leg, or whip—as you've been learning to do in the early lessons in this book—you are imposing your personal space on the horse's space. If you overwhelm him with "pushiness," he will not be relaxed, because he will always see himself as being on the defensive. You will not be relaxed either, because you will be on the offensive much of the time.

Therefore, think of asking a horse to yield as an invitation—*seduce* your horse to move away when you advance (and come toward you when you back up!) Always be polite. Give your horse frequent pauses, releasing all pressure, so he has a chance to think about what he has learned and to relax. Be encouraging even when he stops in confusion, makes a mistake, or misbehaves. When you become tense or doubt his abilities (or your own), the horse will notice right away and reflect your mood.

Give the lightest aids possible. You are establishing a precedent: If you start with light aids, adding more pressure only when your horse does not respond, and then gradually back the pressure off, he will follow your lead. If you start and stay "strong and heavy," he will have no choice but to be strong and heavy, as well.

Be patient, and remember, when the horse yields his body to you with confidence, without fidgeting or resisting, he is demonstrating trust. This is success in itself.

STEP 1
Invite the horse to yield his space willingly on a circle.

- Your horse should be outfitted appropriately, in either one or two pairs of short reins, and with or without the longe or lead line attached to the cavesson—depending on his level of comfort in the short reins, and your confidence in handling them, following Lesson 1 (see p. 86).

Begin at the walk on a circle to the left, because on the circle you exert control over the horse's hind legs when you ask the horse to yield his body. The hind leg you will be learning to control first is the horse's *left* or inside hind leg. He will need to step under himself toward his point of weight as he bends inward on the circle (see fig. 4.14, p. 96). Face the horse, holding the reins and whip as explained in Lesson 1 (p. 86).

You are asking the horse to move *forward and sideways* at the same time. Start with the lightest aid possible—the one you want to ultimately use in the future. Slide your driving hand down from the shoulder area and place it on the horse's side just behind the surcingle (where your leg will be when you ride). Press lightly to get the horse to move away. At the same time, keep contact with both reins. If you don't stay in contact with the outside rein as well as the inside rein, the horse is likely to "fall in" toward you instead of moving away from you. Apply the aid only for a second, and the moment he responds and steps away from you, relax and reward him, allowing him to walk forward-and-downward on the circle (photo 4.15). When the horse doesn't yield at your first, light request, use stronger pressure behind the girth. It is important to remember that you are schooling the horse in-hand on short reins with the same sensitivity with which you will use them when you are mounted.

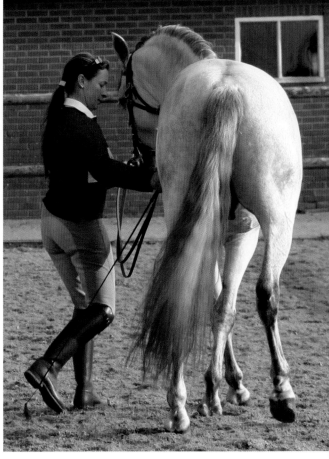

4.15 I ask Fernando to yield to the pressure exerted by my driving hand at the girth line. He is bent correctly toward me (away from the direction of movement) as his inside legs cross in front of his outside legs.

As he yields to your aids, you will deviate somewhat from the circle pattern. You must follow your horse as he yields. If you keep your position fixed, he will have no choice but to turn around on his forehand toward you. Always return to the slightly bending line of the circle to regain the horse's attention and control of his hindquarters.

Practice this first step until the horse is yielding on the circle reliably, quietly, and without resistance. Repeat on a circle to the right.

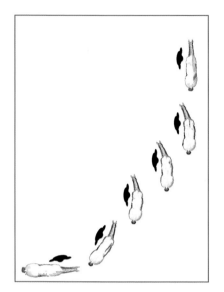

4.16 This illustration demonstrates the yield pattern as you come out of the corner on the first short side of the arena, complete a quarter circle, and then ask the horse to move along the diagonal to the opposite long side.

Teach the yield to the "leg" across the arena

● When the horse willingly accepts your requests to yield his space to you on the circle, you can begin to yield across the arena. Begin at the walk on the left rein on the long side of the arena. As you round the corner onto the short side, begin to make a circle to the left by giving a little outside (right) rein with your driving hand and "opening" your inside (left) rein (bringing your leading hand and rein out to the side away from the horse). After a quarter circle, maintain the horse's bend with your leading hand, inviting his nose slightly toward you with the inside rein, and place your right driving hand just behind the girth line where your leg would be if you were mounted. Keeping contact with the outside rein with your driving hand, squeeze the inside rein with your leading hand and push it a little toward the horse. Turn your left shoulder toward the horse, which puts pressure on him to move sideways, and ask him to yield along the diagonal to the center of the opposite long side of the arena (fig. 4.16). Look in the direction of movement.

● As you approach the long side, straighten him for several strides and then halt. Make sure he stands correctly—squarely with weight distributed evenly on all four legs. This way you are in a position from which you can ask him to yield again.

Troubleshooting

WHEN THE HORSE...

... turns his hindquarters away from you, and/or turns to face you and stops.

Try this:

Lighten your aid; you may be putting too much pressure at the girth line.

WHEN THE HORSE...

...turns his forehand away.

Try this:

Check your body position. You may be putting too much pressure on his forehand, either via the cavesson or bridle, or by walking at the horse's head instead of his shoulder. If you want to move the whole horse, first reduce your pressure on his shoulder area by putting a little more distance between you and the horse, then align yourself with his "center" and, except when slowing or halting the horse, face him with your body parallel to his. He will be more likely to move straight away from you.

WHEN THE HORSE...

...doesn't yield willingly to you.

Try this:

Escalate your aids—here are some ways to do so: Increase your driving hand pressure; however, don't put your full weight against him because he will likely just push back. Point your finger at him, and "jab" it toward him as if you are telling him to "go away." Become very intent in your body language: take a deep breath, stick your chest out, throw your head back, lift your shoulders, and move toward him. (Make this all one quick movement to get his attention.) Tap the horse's side with the point of the whip as you move in toward him.

Lesson 3
SHOULDER-OUT AND SHOULDER-IN

Therapeutic Benefits

Shoulder-Out
- Stretches, flexes, and supples the outside ("outside" the bend) of the horse
- Engages the horse's inside ("inside" the bend) hind leg

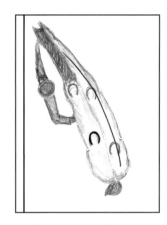

4.17 Therapeutic benefits of shoulder-out include stretching the outside muscles of the horse and engaging the inside hind leg.

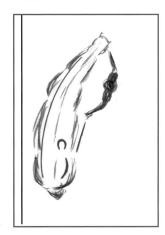

4.18 Therapeutic benefits of shoulder-in include suppling the horse's jaw, poll, and neck, stretching the muscles on the "outside" of the bend, and improving the hindquarters' ability to "carry."

Shoulder-In

- Flexes and supples the jaw, poll, and neck, as well as the horse's sides, back, and hindquarters
- Strengthens the horse's inside ("inside" the bend) hindquarter and hind leg
- Improves the ability of the hindquarters to carry the body forward
- Stretches the outside ("outside" the bend) muscles of the horse's body

Goals for This Lesson

Shoulder-Out

- Further the horse's understanding of lateral movement and prepare him for the shoulder-in

Shoulder-In

- Correct the horse's balance
- Lighten the forehand
- Refine the horse's attentiveness to your aids
- Improve fitness and conditioning

Necessary Equipment

- Working cavesson
- Bridle with the full-cheek snaffle
- Surcingle
- Side reins (optional)
- Short reins (one or two pairs depending on horse's stage of training)
- Cotton longe or lead line (optional)
- Dressage whip
- Rectangular arena

Thoughts before You Begin

The shoulder-in is one of the most important training tools you can learn to use. Not only is it the foundation for other lateral movements, but over the lifetime of the horse, it is also a wonderful way to help keep him fit and powerful, with a healthy, well-shaped, strong back and elastic body.

I prepare the horse for the shoulder-in by teaching him the shoulder-out first, which as with all lateral exercises is an exercise in obedience. To compare: 1) in the *shoulder-in*, the *hindquarters* are on the *track* and the *forehand* is on the *inside track* (see fig. 4.18, p. 101, and p. 82), and the horse is between the handler and the arena fence or wall; 2) in the *shoulder-out*, the *forehand* is on the *track* and the *hindquarters* are on the *inside track* while the handler is between the horse and the arena fence or wall (see fig. 4.17, p. 101, and p. 82). Both the shoulder-out and the shoulder-in are in the "family" of the *yield exercises* (see p. 82).

The shoulder-out is physically the same exercise as the shoulder-in, but easier for the handler and the horse to learn because the handler is positioned between the horse and the fence, which helps "force" the horse to move laterally. In addition, this is a good place to begin with a pressure-sensitive horse since you are not "trapping" the horse between you and the fence.

Keep relaxation your goal when working with shoulder-out and shoulder-in. Encourage the horse to walk slowly and rhythmically. A horse with tense shoulders and a tight body will not yield to a light aid, and the horse must be particularly willing to accept your aids for this kind of lateral work. If he is tense in other ways, that is, he is nervous or he is not paying attention to you, then he is not ready to begin this lesson. Return to the previous lesson and work on getting his attention—and keeping it.

As in other exercises, there are two stages to this lesson: teaching the shoulder-out and teaching the shoulder-in. Do not attempt to complete both stages in one day. In addition, as I explained on p. 80, the shoulder-in can be done on both three and four tracks. *Do not attempt a four-track shoulder-in this beginning work.* Although it is a good exercise for suppling, it is more difficult than the shoulder-in on three tracks. It is considered a higher gymnastic exercise and should only be attempted when the horse is accomplished and steady at the shoulder-in on three tracks.

I recommend beginning both Stage One and Stage Two of this lesson with just the caves-son and longe line, and then progressing to adding the short reins as you did in Lesson 1 (see p. 86). However, I will explain these steps as if your horse is outfitted in either one or two pairs of short reins, and with or without the longe or lead line attached to the cavesson—depending on his level of comfort in the short reins, and your confidence in handling them, following Lesson 2 (see p. 96).

Note: Since shoulder-out and shoulder-in are challenging exercises, consider having your horse checked by a veterinary professional if he exhibits signs of pain, discomfort, or resistance when beginning this lesson. He may have an injury or compensatory pattern of which you have not been aware.

STEP 1

Stage One: Prepare for the shoulder-out by making a half-circle in the corner in order to reverse direction.

Begin by walking straight on the long side on the left rein. Your horse should move forward willingly with his nose slightly flexed to the inside of the arena. You should face the horse as you walk beside him and have equal weight in the reins, maintaining contact as you give and take the reins where necessary to guide the horse (see Lesson 1, p. 86, for tips on handling the short reins.). When you reach the corner, make a half-circle in order to change direction: give a little outside rein (right) with your driving hand and "open" your inside rein (bring your leading left hand and rein out to the side away from the horse). Come around the circle until you can rejoin the track on the long side, now facing the opposite direction. Stay on the horse's left side, so you are walking between the horse's shoulder and the arena fence or wall.

STEP 2

Stage One: Maintain the bend from the half-circle and walk down the long side in shoulder-out position.

When you arrive back on the track (now headed in opposite direction, on the right rein), you are automatically in the shoulder-out position. Maintain the horse's bend to the left that you established on the half-circle in the corner and move down the rail a few steps in this position (photos 4.19 A–D). His forehand should be on the track (with his right shoulder, therefore, "out"), and his hindquarters on the inside track. Play with the reins softly, if necessary, so the horse's nose is tipped toward you. Keep contact with the outside rein so his body doesn't move "too much side-

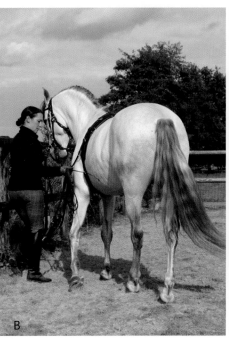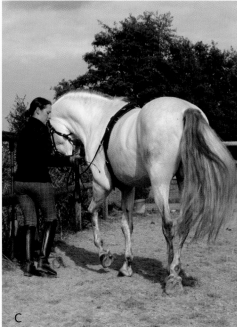

4.19 A–D I am schooling Fernando in the shoulder-out with the longe line attached to the center ring of the cavesson. Technically, in terms of bend, shoulder-out puts the horse in the same position as shoulder-in—the difference is in the horse's relationship to the arena fence or wall. Because Fernando's head is turned toward the fence, his only choice is to move forward along the rail as he yields away from my presence. Therefore, shoulder-out is easier for both horse and handler to learn. In A I am using the support of the whip pointing at his hindquarters to tell Fernando to step away from me. In B, he starts to reach his inside ("inside" the bend) leg underneath his body. You can see in C he is crossing his legs over and moving "too much sideways" (which tells us the angle of his body should be less). The final image in the series shows his next step and a better position of his head, neck, and body.

ways" and "not enough forward." It is a matter of feeling: don't ask for too much bend, and don't pressure the horse sideways—just a little of both will do.

● Repeat several times in both directions.

STEP 3
Stage Two: Prepare for the shoulder-in by making a circle.

● When the horse is comfortable working in the shoulder-out in both directions, you can begin teaching him the shoulder-in. Again, I recommend you begin the shoulder-in on the circle in the cavesson with the longe or lead line, and progress to the bridle, short reins, and side reins only after he's become familiar with the lesson. Particularly in the case of the side reins: should the horse have a very stiff side, he will adjust better if he is not longitudinally constrained until he is familiar with the exercise.

● Start on a 20-meter circle in the middle of the arena. Work four or five circles in hand in each direction.

● When the horse is warmed up and attentive, begin a circle to the left, but now keep the horse's head close to your body while "activating" his hindquarters and pushing them out onto a slightly bigger circle than he is treading with his forehand (photo 4.20). Do this by "steering" the horse with your shoulders—bring your left shoulder slightly back and your right shoulder slightly toward the horse. This pulls the front of the horse toward you and pushes his hindquarters away from you. If he is not bending appropriately, touch the back of your driving (whip) hand to the girth line. This exercise is *like* a shoulder-in except you are making it on a circle, so you can stretch and lengthen the muscles in your horse's hindquarters. The horse should step under himself deeply in order to carry his weight in balance.

4.20 Fernando and I prepare for the first steps of shoulder-in with just the longe line, cavesson, and side reins. I keep his head close while "activating" his hindquarters, pushing them out onto a slightly bigger circle than he is treading with his forehand. You can see my left shoulder is flexed slightly back and I've leaned my right shoulder slightly toward Fernando.

- Repeat to the right.

- Now begin to gather your horse for the shoulder-in. Again on a circle to the left, shorten your outside (right) rein so your driving hand is higher than you usually hold it—even over the horse's neck at first in order to keep light contact with him. (Worry less about actually *shortening* the rein than simply understanding that you need to take enough contact on the outside rein to prevent the horse's body from bending too much to the inside.) When he's going well you can lengthen the rein again and lower your hand, keeping the rein long enough so you can press the back of your driving hand (holding the right rein and whip) against the horse's girth line.

- Continuing your preparation for the shoulder-in, as you circle with the hindquarters slightly to the right of the forehand, check to see if your horse is stepping under his body with his inside hind leg. The smaller the circle, the further the horse needs to step under with the inside hind. However, do note that a larger circle—and therefore a less exaggerated step under—is best for beginning work.

- Check your horse's head and neck position. You should turn his head only a little to the inside, and this flexion should come from the poll. Do not twist his head, which tips his nose up and sideways. The tips of his ears should be level; one shouldn't be higher than the other. His head should be at or a little in front of—never behind—the vertical. Many horses have sore or stiff necks and cannot bend correctly at the poll, either vertically or horizontally. So be patient as you coax him into the correct position for this exercise. It is important not to *pull* the inside rein when asking for shoulder-in, but rather *invite* the horse to softly bend toward you by squeezing the rein, off and on, like a fish's gills moving in and out.

- When he is actively stepping under himself with the inside hind leg and bending correctly in both directions, you are ready to try the shoulder-in.

STEP 4

Stage Two: Perform the shoulder-in from the circle two or three steps along the rail, and return to the circle.

4.21 Fernando and I try a few steps of shoulder-in down the rail. His hindquarters are on the track, his forehand is on the inside track, and he is bent slightly toward me. Fernando is outfitted in two sets of short reins: one attached to the bit, and the other the cavesson, as I teach him the subtleties of rein aids.

Begin on a circle to the left. Establish the position you practiced in Step 3, with the horse's hindquarters treading a slightly larger circle than his forehand, and with an active inside hind leg and correct bend. As you approach the long side of the arena, maintain the horse's position but leave the circle and join the track, increasing pressure on your inside rein to bring the horse's head toward you and pointing your driving hand (and whip, if necessary) at the girth line to move the horse's body along the arena fence or wall. The horse's hindquarters should be on the track and his forehand on the inside track (photo 4.21). Take two or three steps along the rail in shoulder-in, then lead the horse back into the circle, praise him and allow him to relax.

Check your horse's hoofprints or have an assistant watch from the end of the long side as you walk toward her. When your horse is bending correctly, he should walk on three tracks (fig. 4.22). The inside front leg and outside hind leg are each on one track, and the outside front leg is on the same track as the inside hind leg, which must be brought as far as possible under the horse's belly, toward the point of weight where the rider would be sitting when mounted.

Repeat this step (no more than two or three steps along the rail) several times in both directions.

STEP 5

Stage Two: Gradually build up the horse's strength and concentration until you are working along the entire long side in shoulder-in.

Build upon Step 4 slowly. Each time you work the horse, add another couple of circles and the associated several steps of shoulder-in along the rail until you can eventually walk in shoulder-in all the way down the long side (fig. 4.23). Lateral work is not easy for a horse at first, and the "stretching" feeling he experiences as he walks along in shoulder-in, especially on his stiff side, may be uncomfortable. If you ask too much at one time, the horse may evade you, and you risk setting up a negative response pattern (photos 4.24 A–D).

When the horse is accustomed to the exercise in the short reins, bridle, and bit, begin and end shoulder-in work on his stiff side, as outlined earlier (see p. 87).

Troubleshooting

WHEN THE HORSE...

... moves "too much" sideways and "not enough" forward (a common problem when beginning new exercises that involve lateral movements).

Try this:

Adjust the horse's bend (lessen it) with your leading hand (the inside rein) while maintaining contact on the outside rein with your driving hand. Be aware of the position of your body, as always, as it creates pressure—you may be too close or too aggressive in your stance. (Of course, on the other hand, if you are too far from the horse, he probably will not yield enough!)

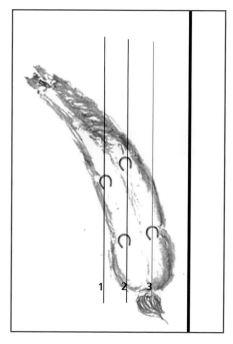

4.22 In the three-track shoulder-in—the exercise most commonly practiced as it is required in dressage competition—the outside hind leg should be on one track, the inside foreleg should be on another track, and the inside hind and outside foreleg should tread on a third.

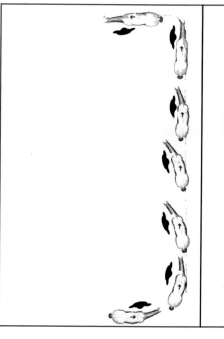

4.23 The pattern for shoulder-in down the long side of the arena.

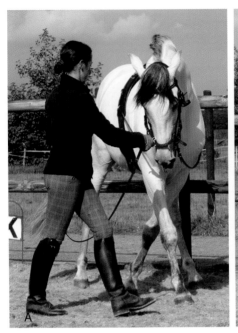   

4.24 A–D As we practice shoulder-in down the rail on the right rein, Fernando resists me a little at first (this is hard work!) In A, he's overflexed with his head down; in B he tries to evade by pulling his head up (note the tension on the inside side rein). Photos C and D show him correctly positioned for the exercise. In all four, we were working with just the longe line attached to the cavesson, in preparation for practicing the lesson in short reins.

WHEN THE HORSE...

...tries to hurry, bolt, or rush.

Try this:

Take a few steps back and reestablish the "brakes" (see p. 72). Your horse may be afraid of the unknown, or maybe he is just disobedient—either way, in all exercises with short reins, it is very important the horse knows how to halt properly so you can reduce speed or stop at any time.

WHEN THE HORSE...

... refuses to bend in the correct direction on his stiff side.

Try this:

Use your rein contact to prevent him from bending in the wrong direction. Then, over a few weeks, gently ask him to bend correctly, a little more and for a little longer each day. Be patient.

WHEN THE HORSE...

... thinks you want him to circle when you are on the track because you are bending his head to the inside.

Try this:

Go back on a circle, and perform a yield to the "leg" (see p. 96), which he should do well and willingly since you perfected it in Lesson 2 before proceeding the Lesson 3! Yield out of the circle and back to the long side of the arena, until his hindquarters are on the track. Adjust his bend with your leading hand. Squeeze the inside rein ("inside" the bend) while maintaining contact with your driving hand, and proceed down the rail in shoulder-in.

WHEN THE HORSE...

... has trouble staying on the rail in shoulder-in on his stiff side, and keeps falling in toward you.

Try this:

Go back to suppling him on the circle in the shoulder-in position (see p. 106) as he is not yet ready for the bending and stretching required on the straightaway. The circle exercise is a milder version of the shoulder-in and can help you control your horse more easily, so that he stretches the correct parts of his body.

Lesson 4
HALF-PASS

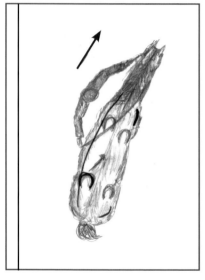

4.25 Therapeutic benefits of the half-pass include strengthening the horse's hindquarters, back, and loins, improving his balance, and furthering his ability to step underneath himself with his outside hind leg.

Therapeutic Benefits

- Strengthens the horse's hindquarters, back, and loins
- Supples the forehand since the outside shoulder must stretch so the outside front leg can cross over the inside front leg
- Improves the horse's balance
- Furthers his ability to step deeply underneath his body with his outside ("outside" the bend) hind leg

Goals for This Lesson

- Strengthen the hindquarters in preparation for collection and carrying a rider
- Condition the horse for performing the half-pass under a rider
- Prepare for the renvers in-hand (p. 118)

Necessary Equipment

- Working cavesson
- Bridle with the full-cheek snaffle
- Surcingle
- Side reins (optional)
- Short reins (one or two pairs depending on horse's stage of training)
- Cotton longe or lead line (optional)
- Dressage whip
- Rectangular arena

Thoughts before You Begin

In the previous two lessons, you taught your horse to yield to you and show respect for the pressure of your presence at his side, and for the eventual pressure of your leg. Like the yield to the "leg" (see p. 96), the half-pass is a two-track exercise in which the horse moves forward and sideways in a diagonal line across the arena. His outside legs cross in front of his inside legs and the forehand slightly precedes the hindquarters. Unlike the yield, the horse bends toward the direction of the movement and away from the handler (figs. 4.26 A & B). The goal of the correct half-pass is to move forward and sideways at the same time, at the angle appropriate for the horse's training and condition.

Note: in ridden work, which is different because we can affect the horse with our weight and balance, travers (see p. 122) is often considered a good introduction to the half-pass. However, I feel that in-hand, it is easier to perform the half-pass at this point in the progression (directly following shoulder-in) because the horse has just learned the yield to the "leg" (see p. 96) and the only thing you have to do is change his bend a little bit to achieve the half-pass.

By now you and your horse should be comfortable working in short reins. Use either or one or two pairs, attached to the cavesson, bridle, or both, for this lesson.

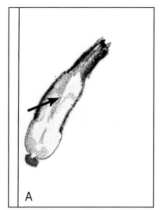 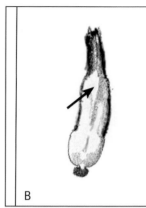

4.26 A & B Compare the half-pass (A) to the yield to the "leg" (B). In both, the forehand precedes the hindquarters as the horse moves on two tracks across the diagonal—the difference is in the horse's bend as related to the direction of movement indicated by the arrow.

STEP 1

Make a half-circle in the first corner of the short side of the arena.

As always, begin on the left rein and walk down the long side of the arena. When you reach the first corner of the short side, make a half-circle by opening your inside (left) rein and "giving" slightly with your outside (right) rein. The reason I make a half-circle here when introducing this exercise is because it slows the horse and he learns to associate the half-circle with being required to concentrate.

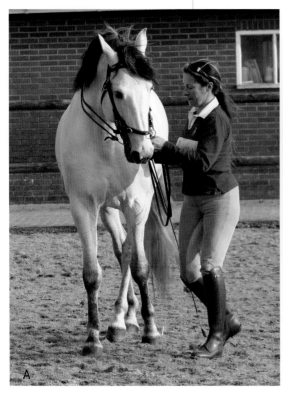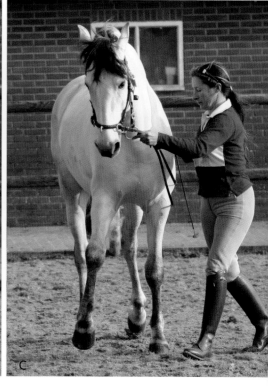

4.27 A–C I begin across the diagonal with a few steps of yield to the "leg" (Fernando is bent toward me in A), then I straighten him for a step or two as shown in B, and change his bend to that required for the half-pass (away from me, as in C). Note the difference in my leading hand and upper body position in photos A and C.

STEP 2

Prepare with the yield, then half-pass toward the opposite long side.

● From the half circle, turn down the centerline. Walk straight a few steps, and then ask the horse to yield a few steps toward the long side (see p. 96). Go straight for a few steps, and then yield again. Repeat until you've reached the long side and allow the horse to relax forward-and-downward as you proceed around the arena.

When you feel your horse is relaxed and paying attention, again approach the short side of the arena and complete a half-circle in the corner, turn down the centerline and start again. This time, do a few steps of yield, go straight for a few steps, and then, while walking, change the horse's bend from that required for the yield (*toward* you) to that required for the half-pass (*away* from you), by turning your left shoulder forward toward the horse, looking in the direction of movement, and lightly pushing your left hand away from you toward the far side of the arena (photos 4.27 A–C and fig. 4.28). "Spread" your arms so your leading (left) hand sends his head away, and your driving (right) hand guides the hindquarters. Your right hand also shortens the right (now "inside") rein to flex the horse's head in the direction of movement. However, keep this hand low so you can press behind the girth line to request the half-pass while at the same holding your whip so it "points" at the horse's hindquarters, which helps drive him both forward and sideways. Stay close to his shoulder.

The angle of your half-pass should be shallow, at first. The steeper the angle, the stronger the horse's outside ("outside" the bend) hind leg needs to be.

STEP 3

Straighten the horse as you reach the track on the long side, make another half-circle at the next corner, and repeat the exercise across the opposite diagonal.

Proceed in a half-pass on a diagonal line to the track on the long side of the arena, straighten the horse, make another circle at the corner and repeat the exercise described in Step 2.

Change directions so you work the horse on both sides.

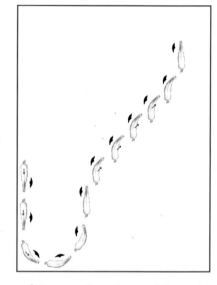

4.28 The pattern for coming out of a half-circle in the first corner of the short side of the arena, taking a few steps in yield to the "leg," straightening, and proceeding across the diagonal in half-pass.

STEP 4

Advanced work: Half-pass—straight—shoulder-in, and repeat.

● Once the horse is comfortable with the half-pass across the diagonal, combine it with the shoulder-in (see p. 101) to further develop the horse's flexibility and obedience. It can be very enjoyable for you and the horse to play with this change of bending in a graceful, relaxed way. It can seem very much like a dance.

● As before, begin with a half-circle in the first corner on the short side of the arena and move onto the centerline. Ask for the half-pass and proceed across the diagonal to the track on the long side, straighten your horse for a few steps, and then bend him to the inside of the arena—moving his forehand onto the inside track—for a light shoulder-in. Be relaxed, but remember that precision is a goal. You may find that making the horse straight between movements is a bit more difficult than you expected, but keep practicing.

● As always, change direction so you work the horse on both sides of his body.

Troubleshooting

WHEN THE HORSE...

...moves "too much" forward and "not enough" sideways.

Try this:

Use your driving hand in the rhythm of the horse's steps. If, for example, you are half-passing to the right, give the aid behind the girth line at the moment his right front foot leaves the ground—this is the moment you encourage his left hind foot to lift.

WHEN THE HORSE...

...tilts his head instead of bending properly (his mouth points toward the direction of movement, but his ears point away from it).

Try this:

Reduce the amount of bend you are asking him for; it is too difficult for the horse at this point. It is preferable to move forward and sideways with less bend than to allow the horse to continue with a tilted head.

WHEN THE HORSE...

...rushes forward.

Try this:

Half-halt to gently slow the horse: squeeze your hands so they alternately open and close on the reins until he pays attention and the correct pace is reached. Maintain contact with the inside rein ("inside" the bend) to encourage him to move laterally as well as forward.

WHEN THE HORSE...

... leads too much with his forehand.

Try this:

In the half-pass, the forehand is supposed to lead the hindquarters; however, it is not uncommon for a young or inexperienced horse to allow his hindquarters to "fall out" toward you. In such cases, the horse is not stepping under himself as desired. Correct the position of the forehand with the outside rein ("outside" the bend), create pressure behind the girth line with your driving hand, and if necessary, hold the whip horizontally along the side of the horse—without touching him—to provide extra support.

WHEN THE HORSE...

... "falls" toward the track on the long side of the arena, as if the rail is a magnet.

Try this:

Practice the half-pass from quarter-line to quarter-line in the middle of the arena, rather than out to the rail.

Lesson 5
RENVERS (HAUNCHES-OUT)

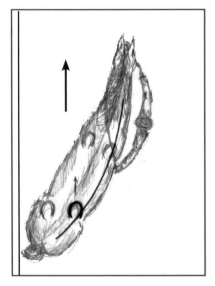

4.29 Therapeutic benefits of renvers (haunches-out) include improving the mobility of the hindquarters and engaging the horse's outside hind leg.

Therapeutic Benefits

- Engages the outside ("outside" the bend) hind leg
- Stretches, supples, and improves the mobility of the hindquarters
- Provides a good gymnastic counterbalance to the shoulder-in (see p. 101)

Goals for This Lesson

- Improve the horse's concentration
- Create mental and physical flexibility
- Further develop obedience
- Complement the half-pass with an additional exercise requiring similar bending and movement away from the handler

Necessary Equipment

- Working cavesson
- Bridle with the full-cheek snaffle
- Surcingle
- Side reins (optional)
- Short reins (one or two pairs depending on horse's stage of training)
- Cotton longe or lead line (optional)
- Dressage whip
- Rectangular arena

Thoughts before You Begin

Renvers is a logical follow-up and complement to the half-pass (see p. 112) because the horse is again asked to bend away from the handler, toward the direction of movement. However, more importantly, you and your horse must have mastered the shoulder-in (see p. 101) before attempting renvers (or travers, which you will learn in the next lesson).

As I explained on p. 84, in renvers, the horse's hindquarters are on the track and the forehand is on the inside track. His inside hind leg is on one track, his outside hind leg and inside foreleg are on a second track, and his outside foreleg is on a third track. The horse is bent away from the handler, toward the direction of movement (down the rail, fig. 4.30 A)—the handler walks on the outside of the horse's bend. In contrast, shoulder-in has the hindquarters on the track and the forehand on the inside track, but the horse is bent toward the handler and away from the direction of movement (fig. 4.30 B). The horse is again on three tracks (unless you are performing the four-track shoulder-in, see p. 80).

As you can see, renvers—although a similar exercise to shoulder-in—offers very different stretching and suppling benefits. It is the beginning of being able to bend and move your horse in whichever direction you wish.

STEP 1

Half-pass across the diagonal from the middle of the short side of the arena to the long side.

- From the middle of a short side of the arena, on the left rein, turn down the centerline and half-pass (see p. 112) across the diagonal to the track on the long side.

STEP 2

Change the angle of the horse when you reach the long side.

- As you reach the track on the long side, position the horse's hindquarters on the track and his forehand on the inside track. You will do this by making a tiny "pivot" on the forehand, "send-

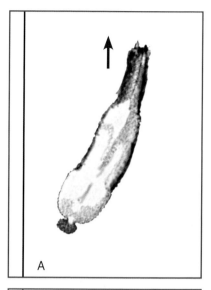

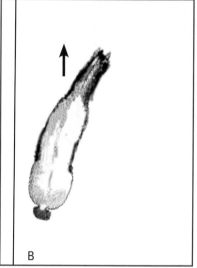

4.30 A & B It is important that your horse master the shoulder-in (see p. 101) before you attempt renvers. Both exercises have the hindquarters on the track and the forehand on the inside track—the difference is in the horse's bend as related to the direction of movement as indicated by the arrow.

I teach a student what the renvers feels like. Fernando is positioned with his hindquarters on the track, his forehand on the inside track, and a slight bend in the direction of travel (down the rail). Notice my shoulders, which are turning to the left to align with my hips and match Fernando's shoulders.

ing away" the hindquarters with your driving (right) hand behind the girth line and the whip held horizontally, parallel to the horse's body. Gently flex the horse's head away from you and toward the arena fence or wall with an additional aid from your driving hand, which holds the new inside rein (note: before the change of in bend, this was the *outside* rein). Remember: the renvers bend is the same as that of the half-pass. Keep your arms "spread" and turn your shoulders to the left (photo 4.31). Think to yourself that *your* shoulders are *his* shoulders. Your driving hand is positioned slightly behind the girth line, applying "leg" pressure as necessary to encourage the horse to move forward and sideways down the rail.

STEP 3
Maintain renvers for a few steps, then straighten the horse, and end on the long side with shoulder-in.

● Continue in renvers for a few steps, watching the horse for signs of tension (or relaxation). Check his head position (see p. 129). When you are satisfied that he is relaxed and correct, change from the renvers to the shoulder-in. To change the bend, "give" with the inside (right) rein and "take" up the outside (left) rein, as if you were steering a bicycle. The horse's hindquarters should stay on track and his forehand on the inside track—only the bend changes so you are suddenly on the *inside,* rather than the *outside* of the horse's bend.

● Straighten the horse before the corner, and begin the exercise again on the short side. Work in both directions.

STEP 4
Alternate shoulder-in and renvers along the long side of the arena.

● An excellent suppling exercise is to change between shoulder-in and renvers as you work around the entire arena. Beginning on the long side, establish a straight forward walk and when you are ready, ask for a few steps of shoulder-in, then a few steps of renvers, then a few steps of shoulder-in, and so on, until you reach the end of the long side (fig. 4.32). Reward your horse with a walk in the long-and-low position.

Work in both directions.

Troubleshooting

WHEN THE HORSE...

... evades the bend by tilting his head or going behind the vertical.

Try this:

His neck may be stiff. Do more shoulder-in on a circle (see p. 106), paying particular attention to his stiff side. Be content with the slightest bend when beginning this lesson. It is better for the horse to take a few good steps, demonstrating a willingness to bend as you wish (even if it isn't quite enough) than to push the horse into a pattern of evasion.

WHEN THE HORSE...

...will not bend away from you.

Try this:

You may have experienced this same problem when teaching him the half-pass. The horse likely does not want to bend away from you because he cannot see you—in a sense, you are giv-ing the aids "behind his back," which may confuse him and make him feel insecure. When you lose the bend, the exercise will get tense. Don't fight with the horse. Instead be creative. Go back to the shoulder-in (see p. 101) to remind him that he must move away from you when you ask. (When the horse loses confidence, always go back to what he knows well or other basic exercises with which he feels secure. From there, you can build back up to the point where he became unsure.) Or, take him on a small circle, and convince him that you were not trying to have him do a renvers at all, but just a plain old circle. He needs time to build his confidence.

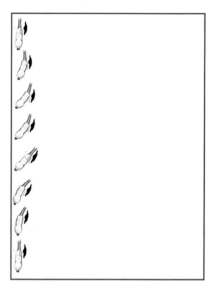

4.32 The pattern for shoulder-in-to-renvers on the long side of the arena.

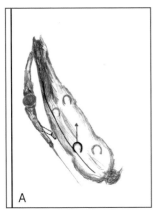

A

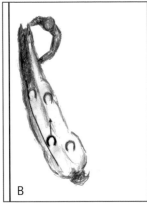

B

4.33 A & B Therapeutic benefits of the travers (haunches-in) include improving the mobility of the hindquarters and engaging the horse's outside hind leg. Further, these illustrations also depict both the starting position I recommend for introducing the travers in-hand (A), and the traditional stance for further travers training in short reins (B).

Lesson 6
TRAVERS (HAUNCHES-IN)

Therapeutic Benefits

- Engages the outside ("outside" the bend) hind leg
- Stretches, supples, and improves the mobility of the hindquarters
- Provides a good gymnastic counterbalance to the shoulder-in (see p. 101)

Goals for This Lesson

- Improve the horse's concentration
- Create mental and physical flexibility
- Further develop obedience

Necessary Equipment

- Working cavesson
- Bridle with the full-cheek snaffle
- Surcingle
- Side reins (optional)
- Short reins (one or two pairs depending on horse's stage of training)
- Cotton longe or lead line (optional)
- Dressage whip
- Rectangular arena

Thoughts before You Begin

The travers performed in-hand is rarely included in training manuals. It poses some particular challenges that are even difficult to describe, which is probably why it is rarely written about! Before you attempt this lesson, keep in mind that correctness and precision is very important, and aim for that, but also expect to make a couple of compromises as your horse is learning. And, when you *do* succeed, give yourself and your horse a lot of credit.

As with the renvers (see p. 118), it is very important that your horse has mastered the shoulder-in prior to attempting the travers. Again, this is because the two movements have distinct similarities. The travers requires the same degree of bend as the shoulder-in, and in both the horse is on three tracks (unless you are performing the four-track shoulder-in—see p. 80). The differences between the two are as follows: in the travers, the horse's forehand is on the track and his hindquarters are on the inside track; in the shoulder-in, his hindquarters are on the track and his forehand is on the inside track (figs. 4.34. A & B). In the travers, the emphasis is on the bending and flexing of the hindquarters, and in the shoulder-in, the emphasis is on the bending and flexing of the forehand. The main gymnastic difference between travers and shoulder-in is in the use of hind legs—the travers mainly trains and strengthens the outside ("outside" the bend) left hind leg (which is stepping under the horse's body toward the point of weight) and the shoulder-in trains and strengthens the inside ("inside" the bend) left hind leg.

Travers demands respect and obedience from the horse because you are basically on the inside of the bend walking backward (which is a bit unnatural!) and asking the horse to both bend and move toward you—even though (to him) you appear to be blocking his way. It is also a challenge to bring the horse's hindquarters toward you with no aid from the outside—such as your driving hand in earlier exercises and the leg aid that you would use if you were mounted. Luckily, there is an easier "beginner's version" of this exercise to help you and your horse learn it while maintaining the value of the physical training.

Note: my "introductory" version of travers involves you working between the horse and the fence—be sure your horse is calm, quiet, and attentive before attempting this maneuver.

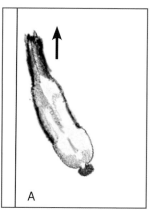

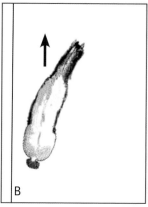

4.34 A & B It is important that your horse master the shoulder-in (see p. 101) before you attempt travers. Both exercises require the same degree of bend; however, the travers has the horse's forehand on the track and his hindquarters on the inside track, while the shoulder-in requires the hindquarters be on the track and the forehand on the inside track. In early stages of training, both exercises should be on three tracks.

STEP 1

Practice travers position with the handler between the horse and the arena fence or wall.

● This is a good exercise to first try after a review session on the longe. This way, the horse's initial energy is gone and he is relaxed enough to focus on precise work.

● Accustom the horse to the idea of the travers by walking between him and the fence for a while. This way, you can use your outside ("outside" the bend) aids to get him used to assuming the correct degree of bend and keeping his forehand on the track and his hindquarters on the inside track (see fig. 4.33 A, p. 122 and fig. 4.35). Your aids should be exactly the same as those you use to request renvers, only your position relative to the arena fence or wall is different (see p. 119). Hold your driving hand low and behind the girth line, bending the horse softly away from you as you "point" your leading arm forward (photo 4.36).

STEP 2

Prepare for the travers with the shoulder-in.

● I am now going to describe a process that you can use to help the horse maintain the proper bend as you segue from the shoulder-in (an exercise he knows well) into the travers (his new challenge). Begin in the corner entering the long side of the arena on the left rein. Position yourself on the horse's left side, at his head. Hold the left rein in your left hand near the bit; hold your right hand with the right rein (and the whip) on his neck in front of his shoulder. (At this juncture, if you feel uncomfortable with the whip, put it down.) As you start down the long side at the walk, move to the horse's shoulder and ask for a shoulder-in for a few steps (see p. 101).

● After a few steps in shoulder-in, move his forehand back toward the track; however, maintain a mild bend—do not straighten him completely. Then ask for a few more steps of shoulder-

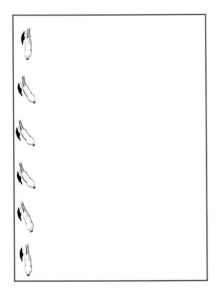

4.35 The pattern for the "introductory" version of travers, with the handler positioned between the horse and the arena fence or wall.

in, and again return to the path with a bit of bend. I like to think of the horse as a curved banana, and the shoulder-in-and-back-to-track movement as a gentle and rhythmic rocking. Continue "rocking" down the entire length of the long side by using a give-and-take motion on the short reins: think again of riding a bicycle—when you steer your bicycle away from you, you "give" and when you steer toward you, you "take."

STEP 3

Make a circle in the first corner of the short side.

As you near the end of the long side of the arena, position the horse on the track, maintaining a slight bend toward the inside of the arena. As you enter the corner, begin a small circle, making sure your "point of return" (to the track) is in the corner. As with the half-circle in half-pass (see p. 113), when teaching travers I always initially ask for it as I come out of a circle in order to slow the horse and get him to focus.

STEP 4

Pivot your body 45 degrees to the right and exit the corner (and the circle) walking backward on the short side of the arena, with the horse bent toward you, his forehand on the track and his hindquarters on the inside track.

As soon as your circle rejoins the track in the corner, pivot to the right and start to walk backward. Continue holding the left (inside) rein near the bit with your leading left hand, and the

4.36 Fernando tries the travers with me in the "introductory" position between him and the arena fence. My leading hand (right) points forward in the direction of movement (down the rail) while my driving hand (left) puts pressure at his girth line to encourage his hindquarters to stay on the inside track and "takes" on the inside (left) rein to ask him to bend.

right (outside) rein in your driving right hand (fig. 4.37 and photos 4.38 A & B). Support the bend in the horse's neck by "pointing" the finger of your driving hand into the "hollow" part of it. He should exit the circle with his forehand "naturally" on the track and his hindquarters "naturally" on the inside track. It can help in the beginning to point his head toward the fence to keep his forehand and hindquarters on the correct tracks. You can also gently push his neck in front of his shoulder with the flat of your driving hand to help him stay in this position. (Remember, do so *gently* because if you push too hard, your horse will just push back!) Continue walking backward, maintaining contact with the inside (left) rein, and yet turning his head a bit toward the fence or wall, which encourages him to keep coming with you. Only attempt two or three steps of travers at a time.

When you reach the second corner on the short side, praise the horse and let him walk forward and downward for a few steps. Try to rely on (and cultivate) your "feel" when you ask for the travers. If the horse understands this new position, there is no need to continue asking him to rock back and forth as you did in Step 2. Simply walk on and relax.

Try this process again in the next corner at the end of the long side of the arena. It may require 10 or 20 attempts, or it might take weeks, before the horse brings his hindquarters out in the correct position, maintains the proper bend, and moves willingly toward you in the travers. However, praise him to the heavens for all his good tries!

Troubleshooting

WHEN THE HORSE...

... brings his forehand toward you.

Try this:

Don't overuse the inside rein when you ask for the inside bend; you risk simply pulling the horse's head toward you and bending only his front end instead of his entire body. It will be easier if you try to keep his head at a little distance from you. The outside rein should limit the bend.

4.37 The pattern for the travers with the handler properly situated in the traditional position on the inside of the horse's bend, walking backward.

4.38 A & B Fernando and I practice a few steps of traditional travers with the handler on the inside of the horse's bend—here you see it from the front (A) and from the rear view (B). I stand a bit further away from his shoulder than I have in other exercises so as to "invite" him to follow me as I walk backward. Here, I rely on the inside (left) rein and the lead rope attached to the cavesson to keep Fernando's bend while at the same time "pointing" his head toward the fence—this helps him learn to position his hindquarters on the inside track.

WHEN THE HORSE...

... does not bring his hindquarters forward onto the inside track.

Try this:

Keep him moving forward with you with active hindquarters, using encouraging verbal commands and/or noises like clicks of the tongue that he already understands from previous lessons. He will eventually understand that his forward energy has to go *somewhere*. He can't go faster forward because you block his forehand with your body. He can't go to the outside because of the arena fence or wall. The only place the energy generated by his hindquarters can go is to the inside. This will take time and repetition of the exercise.

WHEN THE HORSE...

...stops.

Try this:

Be prepared for this. As soon as you turn from your usual position at his shoulder and begin walking backward at his head, he may stop, or at least walk more slowly. Walk on and point your leading hand forward to show him where to go. Keep his feet moving by walking him in a small circle. Make sure your leading shoulder is "open" so you don't "block" him with your body language.

WHEN THE HORSE...

... is crooked (as he will surely be, at first!)

Try this:

If you are working with the reins attached to the bit, attempt the exercise with them attached to the cavesson. With the cavesson you can safely turn his nose to the side using the center ring on the nosepiece in order to bend him (see photo 4.38 A, p. 127). When using the bit, you can inadvertently develop crookedness. Asking for less bend can also prevent crookedness. You can always ask for a more significant degree of bend when the horse is more experienced and more supple, when he will be more likely to respond precisely to your rein aids.

4.39 A & B When your horse tilts his head in response to a rein cue as Fernando is doing in A (note how his nose points toward the inside of the arena while his ears point toward the outside), it is important to stop the exercise and correct his position before going further. Tilting the head negates the benefits of the exercise and can be a hard habit to break. Reestablish correct bend through the neck by easing your leading hand a bit and pressing into the hollow of his neck with your driving hand, as I am in B. Fernando's ears are even and his head vertical, as they should be.

WHEN THE HORSE...

...tilts his head (photo 4.39 A).

Try this:

He does not understand what you are asking. You may need to go back to the shoulder-in on the circle for further suppling (see p. 106). Tilting the head is an incorrect posture and negates the benefits of the exercise, so diligently encourage the correct head position with head vertical and ears level (photo 4.39 B).

Lesson 7
PIAFFE

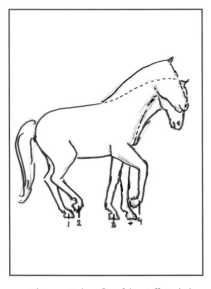

4.40 Therapeutic benefits of the piaffe include strengthening the horse's hindquarters, back, and stomach muscles. Over time, the horse's neck rises and his supporting foreleg position moves directly under his shoulders (see also photo 4.41, p. 131).

Therapeutic Benefits

- Strengthens the horse's hindquarters and encourages them to support the body
- Supples and strengthens the back so it can be raised
- Conditions the stomach muscles

Goals for This Lesson

- Improve flexion of the haunches
- Encourage the horse to support his "point of weight" with his hindquarters
- Train and improve collection
- Free up shoulder movement

Necessary Equipment

- Working cavesson
- Bridle with the full-cheek snaffle
- Surcingle (optional)
- Side reins (optional)
- Short reins (one or two pairs depending on horse's stage of training)
- Cotton longe or lead line (optional)
- Dressage whip
- Rectangular arena

Thoughts before You Begin

In the piaffe, the collected horse appears to trot rhythmically "on the spot" with a moment of extended suspension. But, in a good piaffe, he does not really stay in place—he moves forward slightly (one hoofprint-worth or less) as he steps from one diagonal pair of legs to the other. The horse should move with powerful, "springy" steps and carry more of his weight on his hindquarters. When he lowers his hindquarters to accomplish this, his forehand appears "elevated" in relation.

Piaffe may be taught only after a horse has been thoroughly conditioned with lateral work—exercises such as the shoulder-in, renvers, and travers you learned in previous lessons. These lateral exercises are the first steps toward self-carriage, and the piaffe continues to build upon the horse's strength and ability to collect. It is an excellent conditioning exercise for the horse's back and hindquarters (photo 4.41). It is also a wonderful way to improve a horse's basic gaits—as in the case of my stallion Pícaro, for example. He naturally moves too much on his forehand because of his conformation, and when I first began his training, he did not step under himself with his hindquarters. They especially trailed out behind in the canter. So I developed a program of lateral exercises to encourage him to lengthen the muscles on his sides and strengthen his back and hindquarters. Then I taught him piaffe in-hand, and his canter gradu-

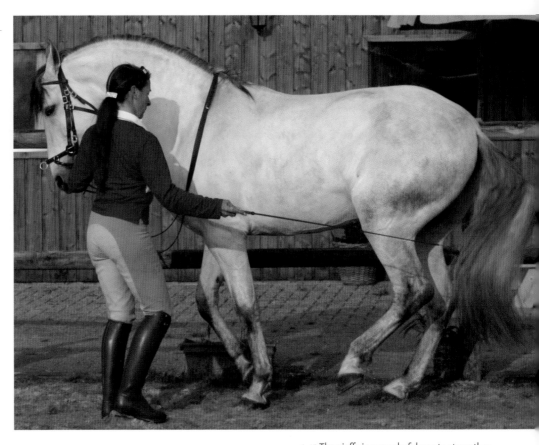

4.41 The piaffe is a wonderful way to strengthen the horse's back, hindquarters, and stomach muscles. Here you can see that Fernando's hindquarters are not strong enough to "carry" the majority of his weight yet. He is leaning on his front legs, which he has brought rather too far under his body. Further work in the lateral movements and occasional progressive piaffe practice will improve his abilities.

ally improved as he became stronger and more collected. Now he has a delightful canter that is full of impulsion, yet is easily controlled on loose reins.

The piaffe can be taught both from the walk and the trot, and even from the rein-back. The psychology behind the different "points of entry" is that an excitable horse is more likely to remain quiet and in control from the walk, while a lethargic horse needs to carry over the energy he gets from the trot. In my opinion, it is easier to start the piaffe from the trot, since both the piaffe and trot are diagonal gaits with a moment of suspension, and the walk is not. Be aware that the piaffe is a very strenuous and tiring exercise for the horse, so it is important to rest frequently and not request it too often.

When he is supple and strong enough to truly collect himself, I think the piaffe is a very "happy" exercise for the horse; he enjoys it. Perhaps this is because it feels like "prancing," and horses naturally prance to impress other horses or express excitement.

A Note about Using the Whip when Teaching Piaffe: Normally, when using the whip during in-hand work, I use it only for "pointing" or I gently touch the horse with the tip (see p. 27 for a full explanation). However, in teaching piaffe many trainers tap the horse's legs with the whip to cue him to lift them. This method has its place—tapping the legs helps refine the exercise. That said, I do not recommend doing this when first introducing the exercise. Depending on the horse, he may get confused from this use of the whip or become nervous. Don't overwhelm him with too many aids.

STEP 1
Prepare for the piaffe by making a small circle.

- Begin walking on the long side of the arena on the left rein with your body and hands positioned appropriately for work in short reins (see p. 87), make a small circle to the inside to reduce the horse's speed and create more "lightness," and to get his attention. Then, one or two steps before you arrive back at the track, ask for a trot.

STEP 2

Shorten the steps of trot with half-halts.

● Facing forward, lean slightly backward with your shoulders and give half-halts—"squeeze" and "release"—on the outside (right) rein. You want your horse to shorten his step, thus encouraging more collection. To help him find a cadenced rhythm, make a clicking noise with your tongue with each step. During the training of these "slow trot" steps ("half-steps" as some trainers call them), I click in time with *my own* steps as I "march" in place beside the horse. I feel this encourages the horse to coincide his steps with my own. (When the horse has learned the piaffe, I stop "marching" and return to simply walking quietly beside him.)

STEP 3

Along the track, transition upward from "slow trot" to trot, and downward from trot to "slow trot." Repeat.

● After a few steps of "slow trot," ask the horse to move forward again at the trot by releasing your reins slightly, leaning your body forward, clicking faster, and raising your driving hand to urge him on. If he doesn't respond, give him a little tap with the whip on the side of his hindquarters to encourage him to go forward.

● Help the horse to transition from trot back to the "slow trot" by taking up the outside (right) rein a bit more. Squeeze slightly with *both* reins to gradually collect the horse more and more. Encourage him with clicks of your tongue to the rhythm of his diagonal trotting steps. You are building the impulsion for the piaffe.

● Repeat the transitions up and down around the track.

STEP 4

Gradually decrease the number of steps between transitions.

- Take fewer steps between the trot-"slow trot"-trot transitions. Ask the horse to make his "slow trot" steps shorter. When he has become sensitive to the transitions, lightly touch the top of his tail with the whip. He will instinctively react by "tucking" his tail, which automatically lowers his hindquarters slightly. And so he begins to learn that in piaffe he must bring his hindquarters underneath him!

- The trick to this exercise is you must maintain impulsion, some forward movement, and a correct, two-beat diagonal rhythm. When the horse understands that he can do all these things at once, even when you ask him to slow down, you will start to see attempts at piaffe. In order to keep forward impulsion, send him off in the trot again (4.42 A–D).

- In time, when the horse is able to piaffe two or three steps, do trot-piaffe transitions. It is important when training this movement to intersperse periods of regular trot not only to reward and relax the horse, but also to ensure that forward impulsion and slight forward movement is never sacrificed.

- Do not expect too much from your horse in his first few attempts at piaffe. When he offers a step or two that look like an effort at collection, give him lots of "cookies" and stop work for the day (his real reward!) It is always better to stop the lesson too early than too late. You don't want to overwork or create tension in your horse, which will result in sore muscles and make him less willing to continue the exercise the next day. Remember, it is very important when teaching the piaffe to be happy with "a little." It can take four to six years to get a really good piaffe because, like in a human athlete, the necessary muscles are built slowly. You can't "buy" muscles...nature requires time to do its work.

Troubleshooting

WHEN THE HORSE...

... piaffes with his tail up.

Try this:

He is not lowering his hindquarters properly. Touch the top of his tail with the whip to encourage him to lower his hindquarters.

WHEN THE HORSE...

... rocks from side to side.

Try this:

He is not bending his hocks and using his hind legs enough, and he is not balanced. Send the horse forward immediately, and return to trot-"slow trot"-trot transitions.

WHEN THE HORSE...

...has lost his diagonal rhythm.

Try this:

Return to the trot and then slow him down gradually to help him regain his rhythm. A lot of coordination is required for a horse to master the ability to keep the cadence regular. Remember to click with your tongue and march in time beside him as he learns.

4.42 A–D Here I begin with Fernando in a slow but active trot (A). I reach over his back with the whip and tap on his outside hindquarter while shortening my own steps slightly (B), which encourages him to bring his hind legs forward under his body and raise his back (C)—in essence, collect himself a bit more. We then move forward in a slow trot once again (D). These transitions teach Fernando to collect and show the beginnings of the piaffe.

WHEN THE HORSE...

... trails his hindquarters.

Try this:

He is not collected enough. Go back to the shoulder-in (see p. 101) and build his strength up before returning to the piaffe. You can tap his tail a bit with the whip to encourage him to tuck his hindquarters.

WHEN THE HORSE...

... pulls his nose behind the vertical significantly.

Try this:

In true collection, the poll is the highest point of the horse's profile. Granted, a few horses are athletically talented enough to collect and at the same time pull their noses into their chest, but if your horse is doing this, it is mostly likely an evasion of the exercise. He is not ready for the piaffe. Again, go back to the shoulder-in, where the horse feels confident, and increase his strength and conditioning before returning to the piaffe.

Lesson 8
PUTTING IT ALL TOGETHER

Goals for This Lesson

- Test the horse's comprehension of each exercise when in a new context
- Instill finesse in your handling of the reins
- Continue reaping the physical benefits of the individual exercises while having fun!

Necessary Equipment

- Working cavesson
- Bridle with the full-cheek snaffle
- Surcingle (optional)
- Side reins (optional)
- Short reins (one or two pairs depending on horse's stage of training)
- Cotton longe or lead line (optional)
- Dressage whip
- Rectangular arena

Thoughts before You Begin

You can now put together the short reins exercises you have learned in a simple but elegant pattern that utilizes the entire arena. Your goal is to execute each exercise with correct form, and strive to combine precision with lightness, and focus with relaxation. It is a subtle balance. Early in your work in-hand when you try to be precise, you may become tense due to your concentration. And if you are tense, you will not be "light"; your horse will be tense, and he will not be "light."

It helps to create an environment that encourages relaxation and graciousness between horse and handler. For example, I often play music when I am schooling horses. Select music that relaxes you and your horse and creates a dignified atmosphere in the ring. One of my Portuguese stallions-in-training *loves* music, especially that of the Italian master Vivaldi. When I play Vivaldi, he shows his delight by offering what I call his "dance moves," and sometimes he focuses more on his dancing than his schooling! So, I have to change to more soothing music that does not excite him so much.

Take your time as you move from exercise to exercise so both you and your horse are prepared and your aids result in the correct movements. Coordinating your ability to focus and relax so you and your horse stay flexible and natural is part of this preparation.

Developing your pattern must not be rushed. Be content to build the routine step-by-step.

Try teaching your horse verbal commands in addition to those for walk, trot, canter, halt, reverse, and rein-back. I accustom my horses to the words for lateral movements, such as shoulder-in. I feel that if horses can understand the words for "Walk," or "Trot," then they should be able to comprehend "Shoulder-in"...and my horses do!

When working patterns, your horse should be outfitted as befits his stage of training, in either one or two sets of short reins attached to the cavesson or snaffle. Use the surcingle, side reins, and longe or lead line if desired. Carry your dressage whip.

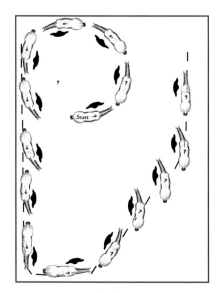

4.43 The pattern for the basic circle, shoulder-in, to yield freestyle in the short reins. You can create your own combinations of the movements you've learned in this section.

Basic Circle, Shoulder-In, and Yield Pattern

STEP 1

At the beginning of the long side of the arena, prepare for the shoulder-in with a 10-meter circle.

● Begin on the left rein. As you start down the long side of the arena at the walk, make a 10-meter circle (about 30 feet in diameter), so that when you exit the circle back onto the track the horse is already bending as required in the shoulder-in (see p. 101).

STEP 2

Shoulder-in along the entire long side of the arena.

● Maintaining the bend from the circle, shoulder-in down the long side.

● As you approach the short side of the arena, straighten the horse so that he walks deeply into the corner and makes a square turn without bending only his neck. You want the horse to be stretching the outside of his body as much as possible in order to bend through the corner.

STEP 3

Yield along the diagonal to the opposite long side.

● As you approach the centerline on the short side of the arena, leave the track as if beginning another circle—bend and curve the horse toward you.

● Maintain the slight bend and cue him to yield to the "leg" (see p. 96) along the diagonal to the track on opposite long side. Your horse will reach the rail with his hindquarters first; keep his front end on the inside track and shoulder- in for a few more steps.

STEP 4

Work at the trot.

● After the horse has learned this basic pattern well at the walk, try it at the trot. Before you begin the pattern, ask for a short trot along the track. Make upward and downward transitions on the straightaways. When he is working calmly, begin your pattern.

Advanced Pattern Work with Half-Pass, Renvers, and Travers

Once you have mastered the basic pattern for circle, shoulder-in, and yield, create your own advanced pattern using the half-pass, renvers, and travers exercises (see pp. 112, 118, and 122). Eventually, you can construct a routine to perform with music, invite your friends, and put on an in-hand exhibition. Your horse will be so proud of himself...

Celebrate!

PART V

Work in Long Reins

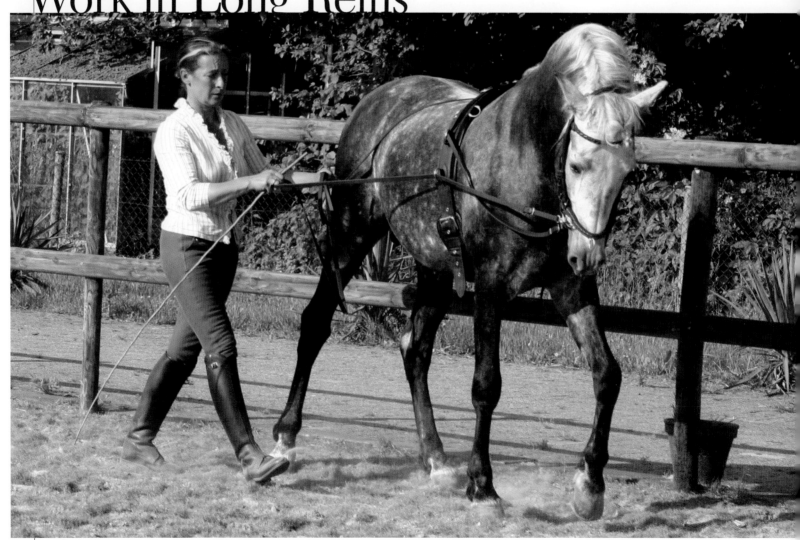

INTRODUCTION

Work in long reins was originally intended to prepare a horse for the haute école "airs above the ground." The long reins allow the horse to be worked without the weight of the rider, and afford enough distance between horse and trainer to ensure the handler's safety.

This work will not feel entirely unfamiliar to you. First of all, the lesson in *long lines* (see p. 69) was an early step in preparation for work in long reins. There are, however, significant differences between working with long lines and long reins, to both horse and handler.

- Using long lines, you can ask your horse to walk or trot on straightaways, and make nice big turns and circles, all from a safe distance. Your ideal position is nearly 25 feet behind the horse, which makes it difficult to ask for lateral movements because the relatively "weak" pressure of the long lines on each side of the horse is not optimal.

- With long reins, you walk next to the horse's hindquarters, on either side. This allows you to use your body as a source of pressure, as well as the reins. The horse learns that he must move away from the weight of the rein against his body—for example, when it puts pressure on his hindquarters in a turn.

In some ways, long-reining is far more similar to work in short reins (see p. 79). After all, you are just using longer versions of the reins, in such a way that you might be riding. In fact, the lessons I have provided on the following pages will not be as detailed as those in the preceding section because many of the fine points of the short reins lessons apply here as well. However, there is one critical difference between work in short reins and work in long reins to point out: the handler's position in relation to the horse.

Position for Work in Long Reins

When viewing a professional long-reining exhibition, you often see the handler walk immediately and directly behind the horse, so close to the horse that the front of his body almost touches the back of the horse's hindquarters. This is because it is considered by many to be the safest place—in this position it is more difficult for the horse to kick the handler. However, this position requires you to be highly skilled in long-reining and to trust the horse you are schooling as he cannot see you there and he still could kick you.

In this position behind the horse, it can be difficult to see the way ahead. Often in exhibitions, the horses being long-reined are shorter Spanish, Portuguese, or Lipizzan horses, while conversely, their handlers are tall. Many of us simply are not tall enough to long-rein a horse from this position.

Handlers are also seen working horses in long reins from several feet behind them. This position is dangerous because it is within the horse's kicking range.

A traditional solution that I have adopted is to stand to one side or the other of the horse's hindquarters, at his hip. I drape the outside rein over his back and hold both reins on my side of the horse. When I am in this position, the horse can see me, I can see ahead, and the chance of being kicked is limited. I can use my body and reins effectively.

Handling the Whip

By now you should be comfortable maneuvering the longe, dressage, and carriage whips, and you should also have a good idea of your horse's level of whip sensitivity. When you are positioned at the horse's hip for long-rein work, there are new correct and safe positions to handle the whip.

The safest way to hold the whip is in the hand away from the horse—so your body is between the whip and the horse—pointed down toward the ground (photo 5.1 A). This is the least threatening posture to the horse.

The first "active" whip position is to hold it in the hand away from the horse, pointed upward, toward the sky (photo 5.1 B) You can touch the horse with the whip from this position, or move it so it makes a "whooshing" noise to activate him.

The most advanced position is to hold the whip in the hand next to the horse, pointed downward, toward the ground (photo 5.1 C). This is the most threatening to the horse, and if you inadvertently brush his hind legs with the whip, he might kick out instinctively, thinking a fly is bothering him. When using the whip in this hand, be sure to touch the horse with it confidently and strongly enough to distinguish your aids from the buzz of an annoying fly!

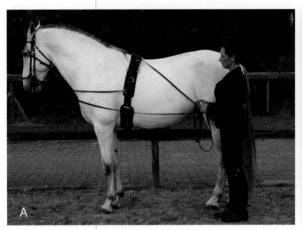 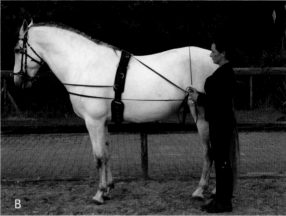 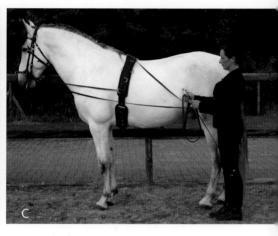

Safety First!

Developing sound judgment where you make every effort to keep yourself out of danger is part of the finesse of in-hand work. Know that when long-reining, your horse may feel increased pressure from your presence because of your new position in relation to him. This could cause him to become tense, agitated, and unsure of himself. So, before you begin your work in the long reins, make sure the basic conditions are there for success. The horse should be quiet and confident—in general, he should know what you expect from him in all the exercises that preceded this section. Both you and the horse should be relaxed. Be aware of your breathing. Regulate it and breathe low from your stomach, keep your shoulders down, and connect your feet with the earth. This will keep you and your horse calm.

If you have a horse that kicks, resolve the horse's confidence issue by desensitizing him to the challenges that provoke him *before* attempting work in long reins. Consider the possibility that this horse may not ever be a good candidate for long-reining.

5.1 A–C In A, Fernando is on my right, and the whip is in my left hand, pointed down in its least threatening position. In B I am holding the whip in an "active" position in my left hand, with the end of the handle pointing down and the tip pointing straight up. If necessary, I can touch the horse with the tip of the whip from this position. The most advanced technique is to hold the whip in the hand closest to the horse, as I am in C. You must be very conscious of the whip in this position, as an inadvertent brush to the back legs could startle the horse.

Remember, when a horse is frightened by something, he instinctively "runs" to escape the perceived threat. When you are riding a horse and this happens—if he is startled and bolts—you can fairly easily steer him in one direction or another, make a small circle, and stop him. When you are next to him on the ground you don't have the same control. Prepare for this issue by beginning long reining exercises in a position a little more forward toward the horse's head than where you will end, to one side or the other of the hindquarters (see p. 149). Because of your previous work in short reins, your horse will be more secure with such a gradual transition of position. In addition, stay close to the horse's side, keep your walk rhythmic and slow, and talk to him in a low, easy voice. If he is a strong-minded, bold individual, consider longeing him before you work in the long reins to warm him up and get him focused. And always judge your horse's state of mind before you begin—it can change from day to day.

Know Your Horse

I've said this before in regard to all in-hand work, but *especially* when you work in long reins, you must *know your horse* in order to proceed safely and truly benefit from the exercises. Let me give you a couple of examples.

My stallion Pícaro is very sensitive and flexible by nature, and he has been made even more sensitive and flexible with in-hand training. He moves like quicksilver, and he can bend every-where. However, there is a negative side to this super-elastic horse— Pícaro can swing his head all over the place, and when he does, his body follows his head in a flash, just like a snake! This means he is more likely to turn very sharply when I activate the inside long rein, to start a cir-cle, for example. He is also easily overstimulated by the increased "pressure" of having me posi-tioned next to his hindquarters. I have to keep these characteristics and tendencies in mind when we work on any exercise in long reins. Since he tends to overreact, Pícaro requires the least amount of pressure and the lightest of aids. Working with him in long reins is both a beautiful thing and a real challenge!

On the other end of the spectrum, although he is just as flexible as Pícaro, my stallion Fernando is less sensitive and doesn't tend to overreact to aids. He is slow, and because of the way he is built, his hindquarters have a tendency to "push" rather than "carry." He is prone to hanging his neck and head and plowing forward, like a diesel or locomotive. Once he goes, he keeps going—even to the point of pulling against me. And sometimes Fernando can push along straight ahead so much so that he looks like he has swallowed a stick! Therefore, with Fernando I must be stronger and firmer with my aids. When he starts rushing forward like an imbecile, not paying attention to me, I have to be prepared to ask him for a shoulder-in to reduce his speed and use his hindquarters to step under himself.

Such differences in horses' responses are made more evident when working on the long reins. However, with every challenge, a benefit lies in the training.

Therapeutic Benefits of Long Rein Exercises

The stretching, suppling, and strengthening benefits listed for each lesson in the short reins section apply to the corresponding lesson in the long reins section. For example, when a horse performs a shoulder-in in the long reins, the therapeutic benefits are the same as they were for the short reins.

Lesson 1
WALK, HALT, TROT, REIN-BACK

Goals for This Lesson

- Develop the horse's attentiveness and precise responsiveness to your aids
- Accustom him to your new position at his hip on either side and to the pressure of your body, the reins, and the whip

Necessary Equipment

- Working cavesson (optional)
- Bridle with full-cheek snaffle
- One pair of long reins
- Side reins (optional)
- Surcingle (optional)
- Carriage whip (optional)
- Rectangular arena

Thoughts before You Begin

Begin with the equipment you know makes your horse most comfortable. You can start with the long reins attached to the side rings of the cavesson, or directly to the snaffle bit. The long reins can be "free" (see p. 149), or you can run them through the middle side rings of the surcingle for more leverage and security, should you desire it. If side reins help steady your horse, use them. Here is where "knowing your horse" (see p. 146) is of great value.

At this point in in-hand training, your ultimate goal is to develop a *feel* for your horse, an understanding of the demands of each exercise, and an awareness of what you really *are* doing as opposed to what you know you *should be* doing. You must make these lessons your own. Now the real dialogue starts. Have fun talking with your horse!

5.2 A–C Begin work in long reins standing at the horse's shoulder in the short-reining position as I am in A, with the inside (here, the left) rein held in front of you and the outside (here, the right) rein held in your right hand near his withers. As you proceed with the lesson and you sense the horse's confidence growing and relaxation deepening, let the reins gently slip through your fingers until the outside (right) rein is draped over his withers or back and you are holding both reins in front of you as shown in B. Gradually move back to your new position beside your horse's hindquarters, like mine in C.

STEP 1

Walk and halt on the track, and travel "straight" in the long reins.

● As you have throughout this training program, when teaching the horse a new exercise for the first time, start on his left side. You will begin this lesson standing at his shoulder in the short-reining position, with the inside (left) rein held in front of you and the outside (right) rein held in your right hand near his withers (photo 5.2 A). Hold the long reins in your hands just as if you are riding, entering your hands between pinkies and fourth fingers, and exiting through the top next to your thumbs. The whip should be in your left hand, pointed downward. As you proceed with this first lesson, whenever the horse becomes nervous and confused, don't push him; instead, come forward toward his shoulder and take up the reins as just described, assuming the more familiar position of work in the short reins.

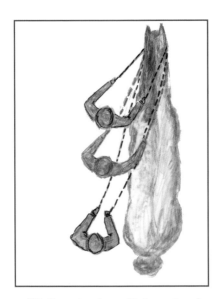

5.3 This illustration shows a bird's-eye view of the three gradational long-reining handler positions: from the shoulder, to the horse's side, and finally back beside his hip.

● Give your normal aids to walk on. As you proceed around the track and you feel the horse relaxing, let the reins gently slip through your fingers until the outside (right) rein is draped over the horse's back and you are holding both reins in front of you (photo 5.2 B). Step-by-step, fall slowly back toward his hindquarters (photo 5.2 C and fig. 5.3).

● Before you reach the end of one long side of the arena, prepare to halt. Vibrate your hands lightly and close them, and move your shoulders back, while saying "Ha-alt" or "Whoa." The moment the horse responds to your aids, relax your stance and open your fingers—your relaxing of body and rein aids is the horse's reward. However, *do not* drop the contact completely or "throw the reins away."

● When your horse is comfortable walking with you at his hip area in both directions and will halt on command, you can address the issue of walking straight in the long reins. Since you are positioned to one side of him, you will find it difficult to walk a straight line in the middle of the arena—at first, you must use the arena fence or wall to guide you. Begin on his left side at the end of one long side of the arena. The horse should be between the fence and your body. "Embrace" the back of his hindquarters with your right arm, holding the outside (right) rein on the right side of the horse's tail, and anchor your left hand (holding the inside rein) on the left side of his hindquarters (photo 5.4). In essence, you "close the horse in," but he can still see you on his near side. This position is the best way to teach the horse to travel a straight line while in long reins. Do note, however, that your horse should be used to contact (such as your arm) around his hindquarters before you try it.

● Practice in both directions.

5.4 When first teaching the horse to walk straight in the long reins, it helps to "embrace" his hindquarters, as I am demonstrating here. My right hand holds the outside (right) rein on the right side of Fernando's tail, and my left hand (holding the inside rein) is anchored on the left side of his hindquarters.

STEP 2

Rein-back in the long reins.

● On the long side of the arena, prepare for the rein-back by first transitioning from walk to halt on the left rein. When your horse has halted satisfactorily, lean back, close your fingers on the reins, and vibrate them, creating a little pressure to get the horse to back one step. Use the vocal cue you taught him in the long lines (p. 72). One step is enough for the first time—build up his obedience, but not all in one day. If the horse will not back up, move up beside his neck, turn so you face his hindquarters, vibrate and create pressure with the reins, and again say "Ba-ack." As soon as he responds with a backward step, return to your position beside his hip. Remember, the horse's ability to lift his feet and bring them backward with the correct diagonal motion has a relationship to his physical condition. If his back is strong and his pelvis supple, he will have a more active rein-back step, and he will be more willing to do it.

● Continue around the arena, occasionally halting and requesting one step backward, and then more rein-back steps. However, don't ask for the rein-back *every* time you halt; the horse will begin to anticipate that he should back up every time he stops, which is a bad habit. (Also, do not *ever* back the horse as punishment. He may start going backward whenever he's bored or wants to rebel—a very difficult issue to deal with in-hand.)

STEP 3

Change rein across the diagonal.

● When you and the horse are comfortable in the walk, halt, and rein-back in both directions, you can change rein across the diagonal. For your first attempt, halt at the end of one short side of the arena. Gather your reins as you go to the horse's head and take the inside rein near the bit. Ask him to walk and guide him through the corner and turn him toward the inside of the arena and onto the diagonal line aimed toward "X." Drop back to your position at his hip as he walks diagonally across the arena to the opposite long-side track. After a few rein changes in this manner, turn him to the inside of the arena and onto the diagonal while remaining at his hip in your long-reining position.

STEP 4

Trot in the long reins, and practice walk-trot transitions.

● Beginning on the left rein, make a gentle transition to the trot, using the cues you have established in the lessons prior. *Think small.* Picture how slowly and how sensitively you can possibly transition to a trot. When you "think small," your body language is "small," or minimal, and you are so concentrated that all the elements for sensitivity are present. The horse reacts to this. When you rush into an upward transition with too much gusto, your body language is strong and the result is a horse who likely takes off like a speedboat at the end of your long reins! You want to build control, with sensitivity and lightness. When your horse offers one or two steps, immediately relax and ask him to walk.

● Gradually add more steps of the trot. You will find yourself moving quickly with extended strides beside the horse as he trots. If his rhythm is active, yet controlled, match it and stay in "synch" with him. If he is irregular in the trot, use the clicking verbal aid you used in the piaffe (see p. 133) to help him find the rhythm.

● Practice transitions between walk and trot in both directions to develop your horse's responsiveness.

Troubleshooting

WHEN THE HORSE ...

...walks "in serpentines" when you ask him to change rein across the diagonal.

Try this:

Work with him again along the arena fence or wall, which gives him support on one side. Also, make sure contact is equal on both reins, before you again ask him to walk a straight line in the middle of the arena.

...rushes into the trot when you ask him to walk.

Try this:

Give-and-take with both reins by squeezing them at the same time for a second, and then letting go at the same time you give him the verbal command "Wa-alk." Repeat several times if necessary to encourage him to drop back to the desired gait.

...continually turns his forehand off the track toward the inside of the arena.

Try this:

Move up toward his neck to give him the accustomed security of the short-rein position, and keep more contact on the outside ("outside" the arena) rein. Slowly drop back toward his hip when he is relaxed.

Lesson 2
MAKING CIRCLES

Goals for This Lesson

- Teach the horse a basic school figure in the long reins
- Accustom the horse to your position on either side of his hindquarters
- Perfect your handling of the long reins

Necessary Equipment

- Working cavesson (optional)
- Bridle with full-cheek snaffle
- One pair of long reins
- Side reins (optional)
- Surcingle (optional)
- Carriage whip (optional)
- Rectangular arena

Thoughts before You Begin

In beginning work with long reins, you do not have control over the degree of bending that you do when you longe the horse, or work in-hand with short reins, for example, so it is a challenge to make the most basic of school figures: a circle. Therefore, this lesson is all the more valuable. Because you are positioned on one side of the horse at his hip, your presence naturally drives the hindquarters away from you as you try to circle. You may find your horse consistently swings his head toward you and swings his hindquarters out—he may even stop, wondering what in the world you are doing! Your first circle attempts in the long reins may be shaped more like eggs, or even bananas. Never mind; just keep practicing.

STEP 1

Walk down the long side of the arena on the left rein and prepare for a quarter-circle.

- Start on the long side of the arena, positioned at the horse's left hip. As you approach the short side, "squeeze" lightly with the reins to slow and collect him a bit, giving him a half-halt with the outside rein, if necessary, to check his speed.

- Keep contact with the inside rein and "give" with the outside (right) rein, lengthening it slightly. Do not "throw the rein away"; the horse needs to feel your support.

- Extend your outside (right) shoulder and hand forward just enough to allow the horse to bend toward the inside of the arena in preparation for a quarter-circle. Balance this position change by bringing your inside (left) shoulder and hand back, inviting the horse to bend and turn. Turn your head in the direction of the bend. Be as relaxed as possible.

STEP 2
Make a quarter-circle in each corner of the short side of the arena.

- As you enter the first corner of the short side, use the inside (left) rein to prevent the horse from going too deeply into the corner, and concentrate instead on completing a smooth arc from end-of-long-side to beginning-of-short side—a quarter-circle. Repeat the arc when you reach the next corner at the end of the short side of the arena.

- Practice quarter-circles in the corners as you move around the arena. Repeat this exercise in both directions.

STEP 3
Make a full circle in the corner of the arena.

- When you feel that the horse is calm and understands the quarter-circle exercise, it is time to try a "real" circle. Walk down the long side of the arena on the left rein and as you come to the corner, "take" with your inside (left) rein and "give" the outside (right) rein as you did in Step 2. Begin a quarter-circle in the corner, and then just continue it, holding your inside (left) rein while supporting him with the outside (right) rein until you arrive back in the corner again (fig. 5.5). Adjust your reins to straighten the horse as you follow the track down the short side to the next corner, where you can try another circle.

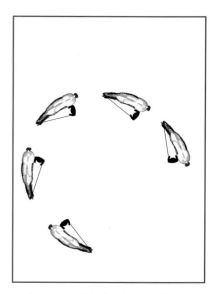

5.5 The position of the handler at the horse's hip, on the inside of the circle.

Practicing your first full circles in the corner of the arena is helpful because you have the additional support of the fence or wall on two sides. Don't concern yourself with the shape or the size of the circle at first. The "perfect circle" will come later. The important things are that your horse retains his calm, rhythm, and confidence with you positioned so close to his hindquarters; the precision with which you give him aids and the obedience with which he accepts them; and the overall control you have over his movement. This is the classical philosophy.

STEP 4

Repeat Step 3, but this time position yourself on the outside of the circle.

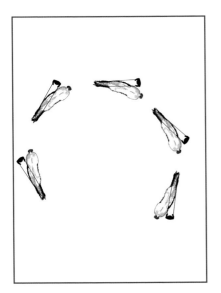

5.6 The position of the handler at the horse's hip, on the outside of the circle.

As you become comfortable circling the horse from a position at his hip on the *inside* of the circle (see fig. 5.5, p. 155), try the above exercise while positioned at his hip on the *outside* of the circle (fig. 5.6). To get into position for this exercise, walk around the arena on the left rein and come out of the corner on the short side of the arena as if you are planning to change rein across the diagonal. As soon as the horse comes off the track and starts walking toward "X," quietly change your position from his left hip to his right hip, adjusting the length and position of your reins smoothly so as not to disturb him. It is important to keep him moving...the solution is always forward! Then, steer him off the diagonal with your inside (in this case left) rein and onto a circle in the corner of the arena—you will be positioned on the outside of this circle.

As always you need to create a delicate balance with your aids. When positioned on the outside of the circle, if you use too much outside rein or stay too close to the horse, he will "fall in" from too much pressure, or he may begin a half-pass or travers. Cultivation of this balance is why we practice working the horse from the outside of the circle.

Troubleshooting

WHEN THE HORSE ...

...tries to stick along the arena fence or wall when you are attempting quarter-circles past the corners.

Try this:

Move off the rail by asking with squeezes on the inside rein, and try the quarter-circle toward the middle of the arena.

WHEN THE HORSE ...

... drifts toward the *outside* of the circle when you are positioned at his hip on the *inside* of the circle.

Try this:

Take more contact with the *inside* rein and walk forward energetically to inspire him to move along with you in your direction and stop drifting.

WHEN THE HORSE ...

... drifts toward the *inside* of the circle when you are positioned at his hip on the *outside* of the circle.

Try this:

Take more contact with the *outside* rein and walk forward energetically to inspire him to move along with you in your direction and stop drifting.

Lesson 3
YIELDING

Goals for This Lesson

- Introduce lateral movement in the long reins
- Teach the horse to be obedient to the pressure of the handler and the leg of the rider
- Stretch and supple the hindquarters
- Wean the horse off psychological dependence on the arena fence or wall for "support"

Necessary Equipment

- Working cavesson (optional)
- Bridle with full-cheek snaffle
- One pair of long reins
- Side reins (optional)
- Surcingle (optional)
- Carriage whip (optional)
- Rectangular arena

Thoughts before You Begin

The yielding exercise on the long reins is not difficult and its value is great. It teaches the horse to move away from pressure and is also an excellent exercise for stretching the hindquarters. As with the yield to the "leg" exercise you performed in short reins (see p. 96), when the horse yields to your cue in the long reins, he faces forward while moving laterally at the same time. The big difference between yielding in the short reins and long reins is your position. When yielding in the short reins your body is closer to the center of the horse's body, allowing you to exert pressure on the shoulder and girth area as you bring the inside ("inside" the bend) rein toward you. When you ask the horse to yield in the long reins from your position at his hip, he will tend to fall away from you with his hindquarters at first. When that happens, you create a kind of shoulder-in—and that is not a correct yield position. The other common problem is that the horse may offer too much sideways movement, and not enough forward. This is often the case when the horse rushes sideways to avoid using his hind legs correctly, and it causes him to "fall over his shoulder." The horse should keep his body straight, use his hind legs to move and carry his body, and not let himself "fall sideways."

STEP 1

Position the horse in the middle of the arena parallel to the fence or wall.

- Walk on the left side of the horse along the long side of the arena, proceed through the corner, and walk to the middle of the short side. Turn to the left 90 degrees and walk straight down the centerline.

STEP 2

Ask the horse to yield away from you toward the track on the long side of the arena.

- Give and take a little on the outside (right) rein with your right hand to aid the horse to move sideways, but keep contact with your inside (left) rein (photo 5.7). Lay your left rein gently against the left side of his hindquarters as a light lateral aid to push him away from you, and turn your upper body and left shoulder more toward him to pressure him to "step away" a little. If he does not respond, lay the inside of your right forearm against his left hindquarter as a stronger aid. Eventually, your horse will yield in response to the rein aid only because he will associate it with your arm's physical pressure. Ask the horse to yield sideways for a few steps, just to see what happens.

STEP 3

Straighten the horse and walk on, remaining off the track in the middle of the arena.

- After a few steps of yield, make the horse straight and walk him forward. The arena fence or wall is a magnet—it has long functioned as the horse's psychological support and safety net. In this yielding exercise, *do not* allow the horse to head directly toward the fence. Keep your work somewhere in the middle of the arena, and work on keeping the horse focused on the exercise. The yield is about establishing a new level of control over the horse's movements.

5.7 I ask Pícaro to yield by giving and taking a little on my outside (right) rein to aid him to move sideways, but I maintain a firm contact with my inside (left) rein. Note the angle of my body—turned slightly toward him—to increase the pressure and encourage him to step away.

5.8 A–D Fernando and I demonstrate the first steps of the yield exercise, beginning on the track on the short side of the arena, leaving it, and then returning to it on the long side. In A and B, we are coming away from the track, step-by-step, at a 90-degree angle. In C, Fernando has almost straightened his body (note his position in relation to the fence behind us), and I begin to ask him to yield toward the long side (not visible in this image) with my outside

STEP 4

Repeat steps of yield, followed by straightening, in both directions, and both on and off the track.

● Continue to ask the horse to give you two or three steps of yield, and then walk straight and forward several steps. Repeat this yielding and straightening exercise multiple times, in both directions, and both toward and away from the track (photos 5.8 A–D). Remember, this is often an easy exercise for the horse—be careful not to bore him!

A B C D

(right) rein and pressure against the left side of his hindquarters with my driving (right) hand. In D, Fernando is yielding sideways a little bit (see his left hind leg stepping over and reaching underneath his body).

Troubleshooting

WHEN THE HORSE ...

... falls in toward you with his shoulders.

Try this:

Be more assertive with the outside ("outside" the slight bend) rein and less active with the inside ("inside" the slight bend). In the short reins, you could use your body to "block" the horse from falling in with his forehand, but on the long reins, you have to rely on the outside rein for such corrections.

WHEN THE HORSE ...

... yields his forehand too much, swinging his shoulders to the outside.

Try this:

Maintain contact with the outside rein and squeeze and release the inside rein to straighten him. Every time you squeeze and "open" the inside rein (taking pressure off the horse's neck), notice that you correct his straightness by sending the hindquarters in the opposite direction. So, if you want the hindquarters to go right to catch up with his forehand, squeeze the left (inside) rein and open it to the left, and if you want the hindquarters to go left, squeeze the right (outside) rein and open it to the right.

WHEN THE HORSE ...

...the horse "runs" sideways toward the arena fence or wall.

Try this:

Reduce the horse's speed by squeezing both hands at the same time and releasing. Repeat. Walk slowly and focus more on going straight than on going sideways. Minimize your aids.

Lesson 4
SHOULDER-OUT AND TRAVERS

Goals for This Lesson

- Engage the hind leg closest to the handler
- Achieve balanced stretching and suppling on both sides of the horse's body

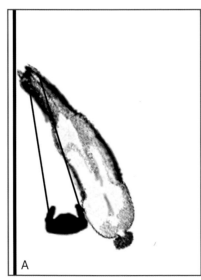

5.9 A & B Pairing shoulder-out (A) with travers (B) in one lesson strengthens the same hind leg while stretching and suppling both sides of the horse's body.

Necessary Equipment

- Working cavesson (optional)
- Bridle with full-cheek snaffle
- One pair of long reins
- Side reins (optional)
- Surcingle (optional)
- Carriage whip (optional)
- Rectangular arena

Thoughts before You Begin

You are familiar with both the shoulder-out and the travers from your work in short reins (pp. 101 and 122); however, we intentionally pair them together in long-rein practice. When you compare the two exercises as they progress in the same direction, you see that you are strengthening the same hind leg (figs. 5.9 A & B). But, since the horse's bend is different, the stretching and suppling effects are felt on both sides of the horse's body, serving to balance each other. It is advantageous, therefore, to change the horse's position and bend from shoulder-out to travers within the same schooling session.

STEP 1

Stage One: Prepare for the shoulder-out by making a half-circle in the corner and reversing direction.

Begin on the long side of the arena on the left rein. When you reach the corner, make a half-circle and reverse direction by "giving" a little outside (right) rein and "opening" your inside (left) rein (hold your left hand to the left of your body for a second). You will end up back on the long side, but facing the opposite direction and positioned—still on the horse's left—between the horse and the arena fence or wall.

(Note: be sure your horse is quiet and attentive before beginning any maneuver where you are positioned between the horse and the arena fence.)

STEP 2

Stage One: Maintain the bend from the half-circle and walk down the rail in shoulder-out.

● As your half-circle rejoins the track, your horse will naturally be positioned for the shoulder-out (photo 5.10). His forehand should be on the track, and his hindquarters on the inside track. Hold the position by keeping the bend to the left with increased pressure on the inside (left) rein and lighter "support" contact on the outside (right) rein. Play with the reins softly, if necessary, so the horse's nose is tipped toward you. The horse will step away from you automatically, since you are walking between him and the fence. You want this lateral movement, but keep contact with the outside (right) rein so his body doesn't move sideways *too* much. It is a matter of developing feeling for the amount of correction you need to make. Continue down the rail for several steps in this position.

● Repeat process in the opposite direction (photo 5.11).

STEP 3

Stage Two: Prepare for the travers by changing rein across the diagonal.

● Begin on the long side of the arena on the left rein. As you round the short side of the arena, complete a turn onto the diagonal and change rein, walking across to the opposite long side. Stay on the left side of the horse as you approach the track.

STEP 4

Stage Two: On the long side, ask for bend toward the inside of the arena and begin the travers.

● When you arrive at the long side, the horse's forehand should be positioned on the track and his hindquarters on the inside track. Because you remained on the horse's left side across the diagonal, you are now between the horse and the fence. Shorten your right rein and "give" with

5.10 Fernando comes back to the rail after performing a half-circle, "naturally" positioned in the shoulder-out. His forehand will be on the track, and his hindquarters on the inside track, and I will maintain his position with increased pressure on the inside (left) rein and lighter "support" contact on the outside (right) rein.

5.11 Pícaro and I proceed down the rail in shoulder-out on the left rein.

the left rein to ask him to bend toward the inside of the arena, and keep the pressure of your body at the horse's hip moving laterally down the rail (photo 5.12) You will likely find that initiating the travers in long reins is easier than it is in short reins because the position of your body helps keep the horse moving correctly. And, once the horse is accustomed to beginning the travers this way, you can easily transition to it from the shoulder-out.

- Repeat in the opposite direction.

STEP 5

Stage Two: On the long side of the arena, transition from shoulder-out to travers.

- Repeat Steps 1 and 2. As the horse walks along the rail in shoulder-out, begin to take more contact with the outside (right) rein and compensate by gradually "giving" with the inside (left) rein. Your goal is to change the horse's bend from the left to the right. Continue pressuring the horse with your body position so he moves forward and sideways down the rail, although now in travers (see figs. 5.9 A & B, p. 162).

- Travers can be a difficult exercise to end gracefully. When you reach the end of the long side, the easiest thing to do is adjust the horse's forehand so he is walking straight on the inside track, and then ask him to halt. Stay subtle with your aids.

- Repeat in the opposite direction.

Troubleshooting

WHEN THE HORSE ...

...moves "too much" sideways and "not enough" forward in the shoulder-out (a common problem when beginning new exercises that involve lateral movements).

5.12 In the travers, you are positioned between the horse and the arena fence or wall. I shorten my right rein and "give" with the left to ask Fernando to bend toward the inside of the arena. The pressure of my body at his hip keeps him moving laterally down the rail.

Try this:

Control the horse's bend with your leading hand, but maintain the outside ("outside" the bend) contact with your driving hand. Point your leading shoulder toward the horse, and otherwise adjust your position so it "opens" the way forward and does not place too much pressure on the horse, causing him to move sideways away from you. It's a delicate balance because if you keep too much distance from the horse, he probably will not yield enough!

WHEN THE HORSE ...

...hurries, rushes, or bolts when you ask him for the shoulder-out.

Try this:

Take a few steps back and reestablish your brakes with Lesson One in long reins (see p. 148). The horse may be afraid of the "new" exercise, or perhaps he is just disobedient. Try attaching the reins to the cavesson instead of the bit until he is more relaxed. Concentrate on controlling the horse's speed and rhythm first, and then try again to attain the proper bend and position.

WHEN THE HORSE ...

... refuses to bend in the correct direction on his stiff side.

Try this:

Keep contact with the reins and do what you can to prevent him from bending in the *wrong* direction. Over the next few weeks, work with him step-by-step to obtain the correct bend. Ask for a little at a time, and a little more each lesson. Be patient.

WHEN THE HORSE ...

... becomes nervous because you are walking between his hindquarters and the fence, and he can't see you because his head is bent away from you in the travers.

Try this:

Keep your hands and the reins in contact with his hindquarters so he feels you there. Talk to him constantly to remind him you are right there with him.

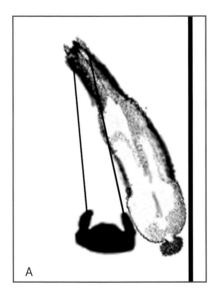

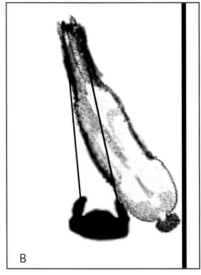

5.13 A & B Pairing shoulder-in (A) with renvers (B) in one lesson strengthens the same hind leg while stretching and suppling both sides of the horse's body.

Lesson 5
SHOULDER-IN AND RENVERS

Goals for This Lesson

- Engage the hind leg closest to the handler
- Achieve balanced stretching and suppling on both sides of the horse's body

Necessary Equipment

- Working cavesson (optional)
- Bridle with full-cheek snaffle
- One pair of long reins
- Side reins (optional)
- Surcingle (optional)
- Carriage whip (optional)
- Rectangular arena

Thoughts before You Begin

Now that you have practiced shoulder-out (and travers), you can try shoulder-in on the long reins, and from there ask for renvers, since it is best started from the shoulder-in. Do not attempt this exercise until you and your horse are comfortable with Lesson 4 (see p. 161). In shoulder-out, you had the extra "support" of the arena fence or wall to help you achieve the correct bend and position; you don't have this help with shoulder-in.

As you may remember from your work in short reins, shoulder-in requires that the horse's hindquarters be on the track while his forehand is on the inside track, and renvers is the same. As with shoulder-out and travers, the difference between the two movements is in the horse's bend (figs. 5.13 A & B). Because you are at the end of the long reins near the rear of the horse, it is a very precise exercise to ask a horse to change position from shoulder-in to renvers. You must subtly support him with the reins and the presence of your body at his hip.

STEP 1

Stage One: Prepare for the shoulder-in on the long reins with a circle.

Begin on the left rein on the short side of the arena. As you approach the corner, begin a circle (you should be positioned on the left side of the horse, *inside* the circle). When you exit the circle onto the long side, retain the bend from the circle, as if you are about to begin another circle. The horse's hindquarters should be on the track and his forehand on the inside track. Put a bit more pressure on the outside (right) rein to keep the horse on the rail, and support his hindquarters with your body position. If necessary, lay your left hand against his hindquarters to help drive him forward and keep the bend. Hold your driving (right) arm just a little higher than the left, so the horse learns that when you take both light contact and raise the outside rein, he should turn his shoulder toward the inside and keep it there. You just created the shoulder-in (photo 5.14).

Ask for two or three good steps, change rein, and practice in the opposite direction.

STEP 2

Stage One: From a straight position on the long side of the arena, ask for the shoulder-in.

When the horse is relaxed and confident in the shoulder-in coming out of the circle, try beginning the exercise on a straightaway (photo 5.15). Use the same aids for shoulder-in as in the previous step. As you walk along the long side of the arena on the left rein, hold the horse's hindquarters on the track with the presence of your body at his left hip. Begin creating the appropriate bend toward the inside of the arena by "opening" the inside rein softly for a second

5.14 Fernando and I exit a circle in the corner of the arena and maintain the position onto the long side. His hindquarters are on the track and his forehand on the inside track, correct for the beginning steps of the shoulder-in.

5.15 I ask Pícaro for the shoulder-in on the long side of the arena. My body position "holds" his hindquarters on the track, I create the bend to the inside of the arena with my left hand and mirror the angle of his shoulders with my upper body.

and then bringing it back toward the left side of his hindquarters (as if your left arm is blocking your own body). Keep your right (outside) hand a little higher than the left (inside) and squeeze it, creating pressure with the right rein against the horse's right shoulder. Turn your upper body at the same angle as his shoulder-in—in essence "mirroring" his position.

STEP 3
Stage Two: Transition from the shoulder-in to the renvers on the long side of the arena.

● Begin on the long side of the arena on the left rein, and repeat Step 2. Once your horse is in shoulder-in, you are on the *concave* side of the horse (his "inside").

● After several steps of shoulder-in, change the bend by shortening the right (outside) rein and "giving" with the left (inside) rein, and give your horse a little space to bring his forehand more to the inside track. At the same time, support the left side of his hindquarters with your right underarm or hand. This logically bends the horse's head to the right a little, while the hindquarters remain on the track. The horse should be looking ahead as he moves forward and laterally at the same time (photo 5.16). You are now on the *convex* side of the horse (his "outside") and you have initiated the renvers. In your first few attempts, play a little bit with the horse's position and bend. Don't try to exaggerate it; be happy if he bends the slightest amount while maintaining the correct movement down the rail.

● After a few steps of renvers, let your horse walk straight on the track so he can relax. Repeat in the opposite direction.

Troubleshooting

WHEN THE HORSE ...

...stops or rushes off when you ask for the shoulder-in.

Try this:

To correct either of these reactions, go back to Lesson 4 and practice the shoulder-out where the horse has the support of the arena fence or wall. Recommence with this lesson only after he is again working calmly and comfortably.

WHEN THE HORSE ...

... walks toward the inside of the arena instead of staying on the track and moving laterally.

Try this:

Move your position from his hip to his side, where you can block him more easily with the presence of your body (see p. 91).

WHEN THE HORSE ...

... is overbent in renvers and "looking" at the arena fence or wall.

Try this:

Use less inside ("inside" the bend) rein.

5.16 Fernando and I begin the renvers down the long side of the arena. His position is the same as it was in the shoulder-in, but I have changed his bend so he is looking ahead as he moves forward and laterally at the same time. I am now on his "convex" side, outside the bend.

Lesson 6
HALF-PASS

Goals for This Lesson

- Strengthen the hindquarters in preparation for collection and carrying a rider
- Condition the horse for performing the half-pass under a rider
- Improve balance, strength, and flexibility
- Prepare the horse for the pirouette (a nice goal for the future!)

Necessary Equipment

- Working cavesson (optional)
- Bridle with full-cheek snaffle
- One pair of long reins
- Side reins (optional)
- Surcingle (optional)
- Carriage whip (optional)
- Rectangular arena

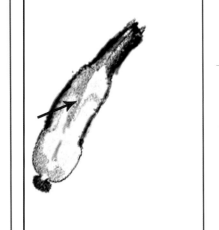

5.17 In the half-pass the horse moves forward-and-sideways while bent in the direction of travel; it is an advanced exercise when performed on the long reins.

Thoughts before You Begin

In half-pass—which, as you will remember from your work in the short reins, is a forward-and-sideways movement where the horse is bent in the direction of travel—and especially half-pass in the long reins, you are performing an advanced exercise (fig. 5.17). You do not have the support of the arena fence or wall as you do for so many of the movements, so you must have control over the horse's whole body. This control is much more challenging to establish in the long reins than it was in the short reins (see p. 112).

Compare executing a half-pass in the short reins to the same exercise in the long reins. In the short reins, you are positioned at the horse's shoulder and head. When you request the half-pass, you can help the horse by turning his head in the direction of movement and touching his shoulder or girth line to create direct pressure with your body and move him away from you. Half-pass in the long reins presents a challenge because you are positioned at the horse's hip. Since you are farther away from his head and his "center," you need more sensitivity and responsiveness from the horse than ever.

STEP 1

Prepare for the half-pass by walking straight down the centerline and turning in a half-circle back to the long side of the arena.

In the half-pass, the horse bends in the same way he did in the travers (see p. 161)—away from you. (In other words, you are positioned at his hip on his *convex* side.) Begin at the walk on the long side of the arena on the left rein. Round the corner onto the short side and turn down the centerline. As you walk, "embrace" the horse's hindquarters with your right arm to stabilize him with one rein on each side of his body (photo 5.18). Try to match your steps to the rhythm of his hind feet.

As you approach the opposite short side, bring your right arm back in front of you with the right rein draped over the horse's back again. Apply slightly more pressure to your left rein while "giving" with your right rein, and turn left, making the soft arc of a half-circle back to the long side of the arena where you started.

5.18 As you prepare for the half-pass on the left rein, it can help to "embrace" the horse's hindquarters with your right arm as I am here. Placing one rein on each side of his body "stabilizes" Fernando on the straight line. Here we are practicing along the rail; next we will try it down the centerline.

● Repeat this exercise in both directions until you feel you have control of the horse and he will walk in a straight line when asked to do so off the track and away from the support offered by the arena fence or wall.

STEP 2

Repeat Step 1, now keeping your hands together in the normal long-reining position.

● Once the horse walks steadily on a straight line down the center of the arena as described in Step 1, repeat the exercise but now keep your hands together in the standard long-reining position, with the right rein draped over his back, even after you turn down the centerline. Your horse must learn to travel straight without the support of the fence or your position (the helpful hindquarter "embrace" described above).

STEP 3

Walk down the centerline and ask for the half-pass.

● Beginning as you did in Steps 1 and 2 on the left rein, again come around the corner onto the short side of the arena and turn down the centerline. As you and the horse walk straight toward "X," shorten your right rein. Establish a firmer contact, but don't pull. The horse should bend softly to the right in preparation for the half-pass. At first, you can tell him to move "forward and sideways" by keeping his head to the right and gently asking him to continue to travel forward while at the same time holding him back with tiny little squeezes on the reins. If necessary, press your driving (right) hand against the left side of his hindquarters; however, try to use this aid as little as possible—remember, the ultimate goal of working on the long reins is obedience to merely the rein aids and the presence of your body. Combine your aids with the rhythm of his walk. For example, whenever his right front foot leaves the ground, click with your tongue and touch him on the hindquarters to encourage him to move to the right and forward (photos 5.19 A–D).

By the time you've practiced this exercise a few times, even a slight touch of the reins on his side will be enough to signal the horse to half-pass.

Ask for a few steps of half-pass, then straighten him again. Repeat until you reach the long side of the arena.

Practice in both directions.

5.19 A–D Here, Fernando and I make a half-pass to the right. In A and B, we leave the track at a 90 degree angle on the left rein, and I almost immediately ask him for a right bend toward the direction of movement. In C Fernando is very nicely stepping under himself along the

Troubleshooting

WHEN THE HORSE ...

...does not respond immediately to your aids.

Try this:

Tap the whip lightly on the left side of his hindquarters. However, *do not* be overly strong with

diagonal and demonstrates a good, straight head position. In D he continues with the next step of the half-pass, and his degree of bend is good, but there is a slight tilt to his head (notice how the tops of his ears are no longer level). Ideally he should have kept his head position at the same height and set as in C.

your aids because when you give a particularly strong signal, the horse will tend to contract his muscles and "shorten" the side of his body receiving the aids. The muscles need to be long and supple so he can stretch and bend his neck away from you in the direction of movement.

WHEN THE HORSE ...

..."takes off" sideways and heads for the "magnet" of the arena fence or wall.

Try this:

Make sure you alternate a few steps of half-pass with a few steps of walking in a straight line so you keep the horse under control and focused. If the horse still goes "too much" sideways, take a step away from him to reduce the pressure of your physical presence.

Lesson 7
PIAFFE

Goals for This Lesson

- Lower the hindquarters
- Flex the haunches
- Raise the back
- Strengthen the abdominal muscles and improve overall body strength
- Teach the horse to find rhythm and balance
- Improve the canter in-hand and under saddle

Necessary Equipment

- Working cavesson (optional)
- Bridle with full-cheek snaffle

- One pair of long reins
- Side reins (optional)
- Surcingle (optional)
- Carriage whip (optional)
- Rectangular arena

Thoughts before You Begin

At this point in your study of the various types of work in-hand, you have come far in the development of collection. This lesson is the culmination of your careful application of the exercises up to now. I hear it said that piaffe is *the goal*. To me this is not true; I feel piaffe is *the key*. Why? Because there can be no forcing a beautiful piaffe. When the horse is in long reins and you are positioned at his hip and he is obediently responding to your aids for piaffe, this is the beginning of equestrian art.

Review the piaffe work you did in short reins (see p. 130). In the short reins, you are positioned at the horse's shoulder and you can "march" with him in rhythm. When you work with the piaffe in long reins, your horse is more in front of you and you do more with your reins than with your body. You must again use your voice to aid the horse, such as making clicking sounds in rhythm with his steps. It is more difficult to keep the horse light in your hand in the long reins, simply because of the distance between you and his head. You must solve any problems from your position back at his hip.

Since piaffe is a very strenuous exercise for the horse, don't stress or bore him by doing it every day. There's no rush; after all, it can take five years to build a good piaffe! (And remember, some horses will never have a great piaffe.) Just do it every once in a while when the horse is feeling strong, energetic, and attentive. And when he responds willingly, reward him lavishly!

Any combination of equipment is acceptable when you arrive this stage. Remember that in my book, *less is more* (see p. 18). In fact, my horses can school the piaffe in just a halter. To begin, however, I suggest working with the bridle and bit to ensure that you have control. By now, the horse should be accustomed to the fact that you work from his hip. Mirror the position you ask of your horse: your shoulders are his shoulders. Bring your shoulders forward when increasing the pace, and move them back when reducing speed or stopping.

STEP 1

Transition between walk, halt, trot, and rein-back on the track.

● Begin on the arena track on the left rein. Ask the horse to trot slowly along the track and click in time with his rhythm. Halt him, then ask for several transitions from trot-to-halt, walk-to-halt, and halt-to-trot. Then request a balanced halt, ask him to back up several steps, and then trot forward. Your goal is for him to respond to your cues quickly and lightly.

STEP 2

Slow the trot and ask for collection.

● Since you have already practiced piaffe in short reins, the horse should have some understanding of what you are going to ask of him, even though your position is different. To start collecting the trot, "march" beside the horse's hindquarters, clicking in rhythm, then ask him to go forward in a more active trot, and synchronize your rhythm. Then half-halt with a little squeeze on the reins to slow him again and keep him beside you, while you continue to keep the rhythm by marching, clicking with your tongue, or tapping him with the whip. As you know, I do not recommend overuse of the whip when first schooling the piaffe in short reins as you must be careful not to stress your horse (see p. 132). However, by now the horse is much more secure in this work and you should see no sign of stress. In the piaffe exercise, the goal is to truly collect your horse; that means, back up, tail down, and hind legs placed under his body. You can help your horse tip his pelvis under by tapping the top of his tail; it is a natural reflex for him to respond by tucking his tail and hindquarters down for a second. Be very careful to use the whip sparingly, and avoid overwhelming and desensitizing the horse by using multiple aids at the same time. (See further tips for using the whip in this lesson in Troubleshooting, p. 178.)

- Try to keep his energy active at the same time you maintain a controlled pace. Each time you transition downward after moving forward in an active trot, march a little more slowly, giving frequent half-halts on the outside rein and "holding" the horse back while continuing the clicking rhythm to keep his energy going forward. You are beginning to ask for a "slow trot" (what some trainers call "half-steps"). When he begins to contain the energy that you accumulated through the trot-forward-"slow trot" transitions, you will see his hindquarters "drop" and his pelvis tuck. This is the beginning of collection.

- When he gives you one good collected step, immediately go forward again. Continue playing with the transitions to keep building the energy and then containing it.

STEP 3
Collect the trot, progressively shortening the steps until they are so short the horse must piaffe to continue moving beside you.

- Ask the horse to collect his trot on the track. Then ask for piaffe with a half-halt on the outside (toward the "outside" of the arena) rein, and at the same time encourage him to go forward by "giving" both reins a bit and clicking with your tongue. Continue alternating the holding and releasing aids to shorten his trot steps as much as possible—and shorten your own steps to encourage him to collect further. The result will be the piaffe. In the correct piaffe, the horse lifts his feet as diagonal pairs; articulates the bend and flexion of his leg joints, gaining a moment of suspension; and places his feet back on the ground slightly in front of where they began. Your horse's first attempts will demonstrate only some of these characteristics, and probably only in a very vague way. However, praise him when he "tries." If the horse has already practiced piaffe in short reins, he should have a good idea of what you are asking him to do (photos 5.20 A–C).

- Teach your horse the cue to "stop" the piaffe. Standing as always at his hip, if you are on the

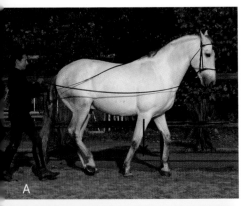

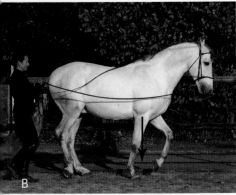

5.20 A–C In A, Fernando is flexing his haunches well and tucking his pelvis as I ask for the piaffe, but his foreleg is angled too far back (see arrows). You can see in B how his foreleg position is better. Finally, in C Fernando gathers himself further and collects more and more.

track on the left rein with the whip in the active position in your left hand (see p. 145), turn the whip across in front of your body and quietly rest the tip on the top of his hindquarters. Cease your vocal and physical cues; tell him to "Ha-alt." When he responds correctly, reward him with relaxed forward movement, or some time in the long-and-low position.

Do not ask for the piaffe often, as it is strenuous; however, you do need to practice it enough to gradually build the horse's strength and ability to sustain the movement for longer and longer periods of time. Theoretically, a perfectly conditioned horse could—and would—piaffe for five minutes straight if asked. Of course, such a "marathon" is not recommended, but the concept provides you an ideal to shoot for.

Troubleshooting

WHEN THE HORSE ...

... does not respond when you ask him to collect and begin the piaffe.

Try this:

Touch the top of his croup, above the tail, with the whip. The horse will reflexively tuck his tail, round his back, drop his hindquarters a little bit, and flex his hocks like he is going to "sit" in the way he should to do a correct piaffe. This can help initiate the movement.

WHEN THE HORSE ...

...trails his hind legs behind his body.

Try this:

Tap with the whip lightly just above his hocks to encourage him to place his legs more under his body.

WHEN THE HORSE ...

...doesn't lift his feet, displaying "shallow" knee and hock action.

Try this:

Tap his lower legs, just above the fetlock, with the whip.

Lesson 8
FINALE—"FREE" LONG-REINING

Goals for This Lesson

- Test horse's comprehension of each exercise when in a new context
- Instill finesse in your handling of the reins
- Continue reaping the physical benefits of the individual exercises while having fun!

Necessary Equipment

- Bridle with full-cheek snaffle or working cavesson
- One pair of long reins
- Carriage whip (optional)
- Rectangular arena

Thoughts before You Begin

"Free" long-reining is known as the "crown jewel" of long-reining exercises because successfully performed, this extraordinary work in-hand is proof of perfect obedience on the part of the horse.

If up until now you have been running the long reins through the middle side rings of a surcingle, you no longer have that security. If your horse has relied on the side reins for support, it is time to go without them. "Free" means the reins are no longer guided or bound by additional tack. The surcingle comes off. This is the true test of whether the horse is fully "trained to your hand"—all you have is two reins, your voice, and the presence of your body positioned at his hip.

In this lesson, problems commonly arise when the handler applies too much pressure, or the horse is in a particularly playful, or particularly disagreeable mood. In all cases, it is important that you remain positive and encouraging toward the horse so he learns to obey you willingly.

Wear roller skates for the first free long-reining lesson! I am making a bit of a joke, but you should be aware that correct free long-reining is the result of many successful training sessions, so don't think it will happen in one day. The first time you try is really an opportunity for you to "test the waters" and see how your horse reacts. When some horses lose the support of the surcingle and/or side reins, they can become anxious.

The tack you choose to use in this lesson depends entirely upon you and your horse. Again, this is where "knowing your horse" is very important (see p. 146). For example, from the very first day I trained Pícaro in the free long reins using *only* the cavesson. I felt he would do well because of his natural talent and sensitivity, and he was accustomed to changing rein, transitions, and lateral work from his time in the short reins. My stallion Fernando, on the other hand, needed to do his long-rein work in the bridle, side reins, and surcingle for some time because when he is in a certain mood, he likes to play tricks and drag his handler (me!) However, now I can use free long reins on the bridle—with nothing else—very successfully with Fernando.

As you did at the end of the short-rein section (see p. 136), your goal now is to link together the lessons you've learned on the long reins into a cohesive pattern. Play with your skills, and your ability to prepare for new movements and concentrate despite distraction. Begin with the familiar and use the same patterns that you practiced in the short reins. Add the following elements:

- Walk a straight line, shoulder-in, then walk a straight line again.
- Change rein, and ask for shoulder-out on the new long side.
- Perform a half-circle to reverse direction back to the track.
- Turn down the centerline and half-pass.

Gradually include other combinations of exercises. It makes sense to start with the more basic elements and work up to the most sophisticated. On the following pages, I demonstrate the movements you've learned in Sections IV and V in the free long reins. Use them for reference as you build your own schooling patterns.

Free Long-Reining—A Lesson in Photographs

5.21 Straight

When you begin a lesson in the free long reins, always start working on a straight line because it is an easy way for you and the horse to warm up, focus, and—if it is his first time without the surcingle and/or other equipment—get used to the feeling of working in less tack. Here I am walking with Fernando. He has the support of the fence on one side and the presence of my body on the other, which helps him feel more secure and less "naked."

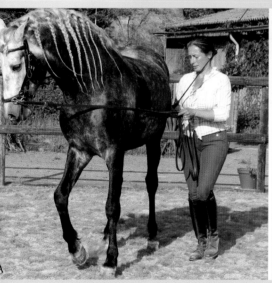

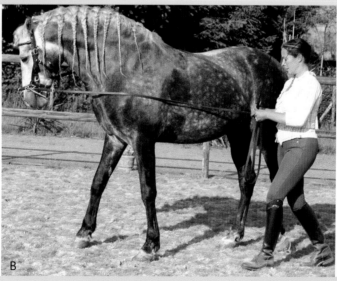

5.22 A–C Reverse Direction

Before you attempt lateral movements on the free long reins, practice changing direction by turning a very small half-circle toward the inside of the arena. On the long side, walk to the end and ask the horse to turn in toward the middle of the arena just before you reach the corner. Make a small half-circle and return to the track, now facing the opposite direction. If you start on the left rein (so you are positioned at the horse's left hip), stay in that position (on the inside of the horse's bend) so that when you return to the track, you are now between the horse and the arena fence or wall. Walk down the rail and then reverse direction again, remaining on the horse's left side. This photo series shows the second direction change—I am on the outside ("outside" the bend) of Pícaro's small half-circle, and I will end up back on the inside of the arena when we return to the track.

A

B

5.23 A & B Shoulder-Out

When I ask for a shoulder-out and keep the horse's head pointed toward the fence, as I am doing here with Fernando, he must move sideways while still going forward. This is an easy movement to start with, for both you and your horse. You can see in the rear view picture how he is reaching under himself with the inside ("inside" the bend) hind leg—great gymnastic exercise.

5.24 Travers

Review Lesson 4 in the long-reining section (see p. 161). There, I explain how to transition from the shoulder-out to the travers, which involves a change in the bend from toward the fence or wall to toward the middle of the arena. Compare

this photo to photo 5.23 A. I have changed Fernando's bend by "taking" with the right rein and "giving" with the left. He has to keep his hindquarters on the inside track because I am walking between him and the fence.

5.25 Shoulder-In

Here you can see a perfect shoulder-in. Fernando is relaxed, his head is in a correct position (bent toward the inside of the arena with his nose on or just in front of the vertical), and the angle of his body (the degree his forehand has come in off the track) is good. The difficulty with this exercise in free long reins is that you have to keep contact with both reins and "check" him (squeeze and release, squeeze and release), continually to keep him from heading out into the middle of the arena.

5.26 Renvers

In this image of a renvers (which is not quite perfect—Fernando could have just a little more bend) you can see the similarity between a shoulder-in and a renvers (compare to photo 5.25), but as with shoulder-out and travers, the bend is different. The horse should be warmed up and willingly completing other lateral movements before you try the renvers. I like to transition from the shoulder-in on the long side to the renvers (see Lesson 5, p. 166).

A B C

5.27 A–C Half-Pass

Before you try half-pass in free long reins, practice yielding a few times (see p. 157). Experiment with the reins to change the degree of bend in the movement. When he is warmed up and attentive, ask for the half-pass. Here I have positioned Fernando to bend in the direction of movement, and I am verbally encouraging him to step laterally at the same time he goes forward. Note that my whip is pointing up in an "active" position to add pressure if necessary. His forehand is leading his hindquarters as his outside legs ("outside" the bend) cross over in front of his inside legs ("inside" the bend). Be aware that when performing half-pass in free long reins the horse tends to move "too much" sideways and "not enough" forward. It is a matter of you developing a feeling for it.

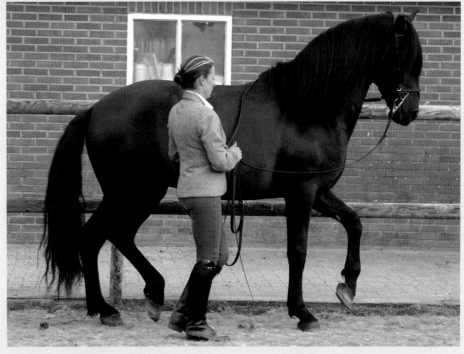

5.28 Freedance!

Here Salguiero offers an elastic trot on loose reins. The only thing I have to do is walk next to him. He is relaxed, and as you can see, he is completely happy. This is the reward—this is fun!

Acknowledgments

First, we thank Trafalgar Square Books for taking on this project that is so important to us. We especially thank the most gracious Rebecca Didier, Senior Editor, who gently coached us through all the stages of the process of making a book.

From Ellen

With this book I want to share what I have learned so far with my horses. I want to thank:

My Spanish stallions, Fernando, Pícaro, and Bodequero. I have also now started my youngest stallion, four-year-old Tanguillo, newly arrived from Spain, having lived in a herd under the olive trees all his life with no human influences on his behavior. It is a gift to see a pure and untrained horse responding to my in-hand lessons, proving they do work! Also, I am reminded that even an untrained horse is not straight. Not only do humans sometimes *make* horses crooked, but Nature plays a part, too.

My wonderful husband, Thom, for his belief in me, his patience and his love. Thom accepts my passion for horses and has helped me to develop as a horseman. He has given me the freedom to go to other countries to train and learn, with and without my own horses, for weeks in a row, year after year. I thank him from the bottom of my heart. Without him I would never have come this far.

My instructors who taught me, institutions where I have trained, and the masters who have inspired me, including:

■ Pedro Baptista de Almeida of Portugal, student of Nuno Oliveira, the greatest classical rider and trainer of the last century
■ Franciso Bessa de Carvalho, Third Rider of Escola Portuguesa de Arte Equestre
■ Bent Branderup of Denmark, student of Egon von Neindorf and specialist in baroque academic equitation
■ Real Escuela del Arte Ecuestre, the Royal School of Equestrian Arts in Spain
■ David de Wispelaere of the United States, student of Arthur Kottas, former First Chief Rider at the Spanish Riding School in Vienna, Austria
■ Sebastiaan Fernandez of Spain, Doma Vaquera and garrocha specialist
■ Jesus Morales of Spain, Doma Vaquera and garrocha specialist
■ Fürstliche Hofreitschule of Germany, Baroque equitation according to La Guiérinière
■ Michel Henriquet and Catherine Durand of France, Michel a lifelong friend of Nuno Oliveira, and Catherine, rider on the French dressage team in the 1992 Olympic Games in Barcelona
■ And all the other people from whom I have learned....

My co-author and now friend, Kip Mistral, whom I have met in my equestrian quest. Never in my life have I met a person who can work with words so beautifully. She is a great horse lover and believes in the same values as I do. She has a pure belief that there can be a better world for horses, and her love for them is very deep.

My mother and parents-in-law, who are very proud of me and love the things I do with horses, although they sometimes don't understand what it's all about. They come to see me ride whenever I give exhibitions and are always there to help whenever I ask them.

My father, who is in Heaven, I thank from my heart in a special way, because he was responsible for putting me on a horse for the first time when I was three years old. He taught me to love nature and animals, and he is responsible for my passionate love for horses. I know he is so very proud of me and I hope he can see me from above. Thank you, Papa, and I love you.

From Kip

A handsome woman in breeches, tall boots, and spurs strode purposefully past me as I stood waiting with my bags in the beautiful Copenhagen airport. Ponygirl! I called out, and Ellen Schuthof-Lesmeister turned to search for the owner of the voice. We were meeting, finally, after a year of e-mailing, exchanging photographs, books, and ideas, but when we hugged in greeting it seemed like we had known each other always. Ellen and Bent Branderup were at the airport to pick me up and take me with them to Bent's equestrian facility where Ellen was studying for two weeks. After the clinic, we drove her Spanish stallions Fernando and Pícaro from Denmark through Germany and back to Holland, where I stayed with Ellen and her husband Thom for a week at their beautiful home and equestrian facility *Stal Paradiso*. This was almost three years ago, the first of several visits to Stal Paradiso and the beginning of an odyssey for Ellen and me, which I hope will never end, as together we explore the equestrian arts. Thank you, Ellen, for your inspiration and wonderful friendship!

My passage through horsemanship has been very different from Ellen's. My stepfather, Max Porter, rode saddle broncs in Montana rodeos as a young man and in his lovely tenor sang me to sleep with Western ballads. He taught this horse-crazy little girl to ride and bought me my first horse, the notoriously tricky Tony the Pony. Dad saw me through every kind of equestrian adventure, and I will always be grateful. My aunt Naomi Libby also kindly supported my passion for horses. Many was the weekend she invited Tony and me to her horse property so we could ride in the nearby desert with my cousin Lauren, and many the weekend she took us along to local shows and gymkhanas where Tony and I tasted our share of successes.

But I am still on horseback in the hills of southwestern Montana in my favorite memories, where I was lucky to spend summers and holidays on relatives' ranches riding from first to last light every day. One unforgettable college Christmas vacation, in 36-degrees-below-zero weather, I helped trail hungry cows from high pastures chest deep in snow down to the home ranch to be fed through the winter and await their early spring calving. Ranch life is far from easy, and those horsemen and the intelligent cow horses I was privileged to ride I'll never forget. It was a world that few of us today have the opportunity to experience.

So I'd like to thank Larry Epling, rancher, horse trainer, and man of the very type I admired so much in those earlier times, who has reminded me of what I learned then, that being a horseman is a 24-7 state-of-mind. A *horseman* learns to see a horse for what he is, and he makes it his business to learn how to communicate with that horse in order to, as Larry says, "patiently and naturally come to an understanding." A *horseman* puts the horse first, every time.

Our hope for this book is that it will invoke that spirit of the *horseman* across all the equestrian disciplines, bridging our individual and collective dreams for our horses and uniting us in one community. May we strive to serve the horse with the unfailing loyalty and generosity with which he has served us throughout our long history together.

Index